TALL SHIPS ON PUGET SOUND

Robert Weinstein, a widely respected specialist in maritime history and in the photographic history of the United States, has selected the photographs in this volume and has written a perceptive text to accompany them. He is the author of several books, including *Collection, Use, and Care of Historical Photographs*.

TALL SHIPS ON PUGET SOUND

The Marine Photographs of Wilhelm Hester

ROBERT A. WEINSTEIN

UNIVERSITY OF WASHINGTON PRESS *Seattle and London*

To Vivian and David, who make all things possible

Library of Congress Cataloging in Publication Data

Weinstein, Robert A.
    Tall ships on Puget Sound.

    1.   Photography of sailing ships.   2.   Puget Sound—
Description and travel—Views.   I. Hester, Wilhelm.
II.   Title..
TR690.W43   779'.37'0916432   78–4372
ISBN 0–295–95619–4

*Frontispiece: Newly arrived from Japan, bound for Tacoma
to load two thousand tons of wheat going to Queenstown
for orders, the full-rigged ship* Dalgonar, *the pride of her
old school commander, Captain James Kitchen, lies in
solitary grandeur in Seattle's Elliott Bay.*

Acknowledgments

From the moment Wilhelm Hester's maritime photographs were made public they have excited continuing interest among maritime historians, sailing ship enthusiasts, and museum curators. From all quarters of the world people have contributed useful information and expertise, making it possible to date and identify these photographs accurately. Were it not for the help of such knowledgeable aficionados the Hester collection would not now be valued as a maritime resource of the first rank. Their contributions deserve recognition and gratitude. Without them the writing of this book would have been impossible.

Too many partners have accompanied me on this delightful journey to single out each cooperative helper by name. I greatly regret the omission of many names and hope that any thus omitted will accept my gratitude for their contribution to this work. As in any endeavor requiring assistance, some contributed so much to the work that it would be unthinkable to deny them personal recognition by name.

Heading the list are Nora and Jerry Sands of Seattle, Washington. They discovered the Hester negatives in their newly-purchased home, treasured them, and persisted in their efforts to place them into responsible hands. Their devotion and energy exceeded all others.

Mr. Emerson L. Spear of Los Angeles recognized Hester's photographs as valuable historical artifacts instantly and generously provided the money to purchase them as a gift for the San Francisco Maritime Museum.

Mr. Karl Kortum, Director of the museum, an effective catalyst for maritime preservation, has generously made Hester's photographs available for reproduction and study. In his enthusiasm for the images, he has displayed enlargements in the museum to great advantage. The skill and understanding of Harlan Soeten, Curator of the museum, cannot be overesteemed. Mrs. Matilda Dring, the museum's Photo Archivist and her assistant, Ms. Danee MacPhee, cared for the Hester plates in their custody wisely and lovingly. Without their cataloging and organizing skills the collection would have remained unavailable for use.

Few have devoted greater effort to the difficult task of identifying the ships and their crews than Captain Harold D. Huycke, Jr., of Edmonds, Washington, and Andrew J. Nesdall of Waban, Massachusetts. Their combined encyclopedic knowledge has proved invaluable. They have successfully solicited the assistance of their colleagues throughout the world in search of information. Their unflagging energy developed many new sources for research.

Robert D. Monroe, Head of Special Collections at the University of Washington Library in Seattle, provided original Hester prints for study as well as insuring a steady flow of xeroxed documentation and endless quantities of translated letters and additional information relating to the Pacific Northwest. He read this manuscript, offered helpful advice, and generously wrote needed encouragement, as well as providing Hester prints for reproduction in this book.

Captain Fred K. Klebingat, retired Pacific Coast shipmaster, provided useful criticism, information, and maritime understanding that only he, a participant in those times, could have supplied. Gary White of Auburn, Washington, secured a copy of Hester's death certificate and supplied information on the Hall Brothers shipbuilding yard from his own extensive research. Gavin Craig, a British sailing ship veteran, kindly allowed me to quote from his eloquent letters. Gustav Alexanderrson of Stockholm sent useful notes on the arrivals and departures of many of these ships, while John Lyman, distinguished Pacific Coast maritime historian, answered my queries fully and promptly as well as pointing out additional sources.

My wife, Vivian, and my scholar son, David, both earned my gratitude providing helpful criticism and reinforcing encouragement. They each read this manuscript many times along the way, rendering badly needed assistance. I relied on their abilities to see errors eluding my critical eye. Above all else they patiently endured my many disappointments and resulting bad tempers. For such generosity there cannot be thanks enough.

Much remains to be learned about Wilhelm Hester's life, his work, the ships and seamen he photographed, and the trades that brought them to Puget Sound. Digging for that additional knowledge continues and both the San Francisco Maritime Museum and the University of Washington Library will welcome new information and corrections of existing error.

Undoubtedly errors will be discovered in this preliminary work. They are all mine and I regret their inclusion. All of those who helped me worked hard to see that I avoided them. So have I.

Robert A. Weinstein

Contents

Little known outside of a few ports these hardened veterans of the Horn, men of all nationalities, ages, and temperaments, comprise the able-bodied crew of the German bark Bertha *loading grain at Tacoma.*

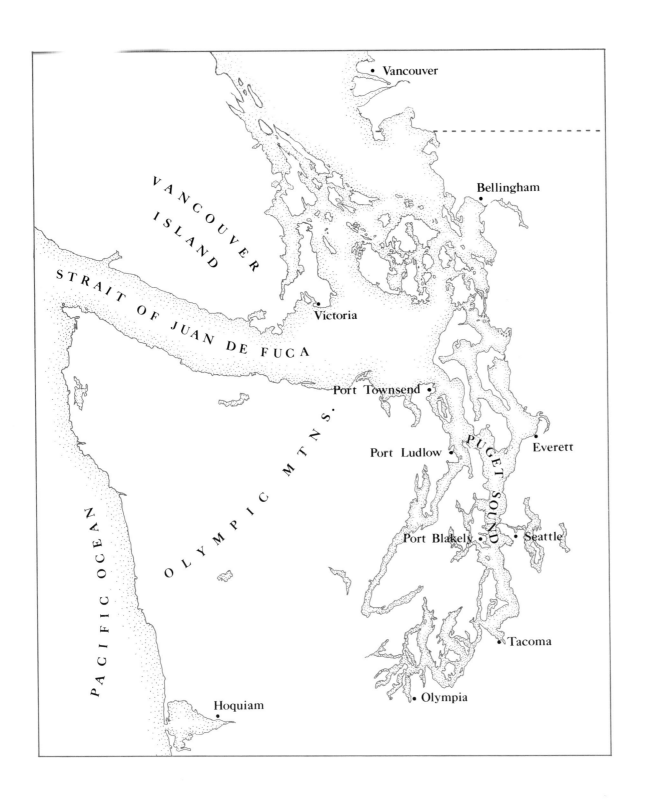

TALL SHIPS ON PUGET SOUND

Introduction

It is a wonder this collection of nineteenth-century prints and negatives, unlike so many others, has survived. For many years it lay, packed in wooden boxes, unused and neglected in Wilhelm Hester's home atop Capitol Hill in Seattle. It is even more remarkable that after suffering summer heat and Puget Sound's wintry damps for over forty years so few of these 8″ × 10″ glass dry plates, jacketed in high-acid kraft envelopes, deteriorated. They all should have.

Although the plates had originally been boxed with care, in subsequent years the collection was scattered through many rooms of Hester's house. There it lay, neither organized nor catalogued, stacked along with sundry boxes and barrels in random disorder. Nor was it secured from dirt, damp, or insects. The individual wooden boxes that housed the collection were not tagged as containing photographic plates, nor were the sagging cardboard cartons piled high with Hester's mounted prints. They might easily have been thrown out by an uncomprehending person trying to bring order to the dusty, crowded rooms.

After Hester's death in 1947 his house was purchased by Jerry and Nora Sands. These two people more than any others were responsible for saving Hester's photographs and negatives. Clearing up their new home the Sands eventually stumbled onto the wooden boxes containing approximately 1,350

Winter snows dress Blakely's forested shore, blanketing the quiet mill wharf. Tall ships rock slowly in the hushed cold, tugging at the frosty hawsers binding them to the land.

of Hester's negatives. Intuitively they sensed their importance as rare historical artifacts. After cleaning the dirt-encrusted envelopes in which the plates were jacketed they pulled together as much of the collection as they could find and stored it in cooler circumstances.

The Sands were determined to find a responsible home for Hester's plates. They realized they should not try to keep them themselves. Putting together a local institution and a benevolent donor to purchase the collection was their goal.

Word of the collection's existence was passed discreetly among interested parties in Seattle and several individuals inspected it. In spite of appreciation for its evident worth the Sands received *no* offer worthy of serious consideration. It appeared that those who wanted the Hester negatives hoped to buy them for next to nothing. The owners of the plates were badly shaken by these initial responses.

As time went by, the Sands broadened their efforts to interest out-of-state buyers. Even certain carefully selected individuals in other countries were told about the Hester collection and a few of them came to see it. But all of these efforts failed and the Sands became disheartened. They were certain Hester's photographs were an important record of Puget Sound shipping, sure as well that they should be preserved in some fashion.

Gordon Jones, a Pacific Coast maritime historian, drew my attention to the collection. I wrote to the Sands in 1960 and encouraged them to send a group of specimen plates to me in Los Angeles, so I could inspect the plates and print several of the images. The contact prints from these 8″ × 10″ glass negatives verified in vivid detail their importance. It was clear they were not only valuable but unique.

I then showed the prints to Mr. Emerson Spear

of Los Angeles, the grandson of Captain Alexander Spear, who came around the Horn to San Francisco in Gold Rush days. His appreciation of the collection and recognition of its historic value was both certain and swift. The San Francisco Maritime Museum's Board of Trustees was delighted to accept his offer to purchase it as a gift to honor the memory of his sailor grandfather.

Immediate negotiations by mail ensued for their purchase and were concluded by swift agreement on a suitable price. Acting as Mr. Spear's agent I flew to Seattle, inspected the balance of the collection, secured a bill of sale, and supervised the careful packing of the collection for shipment to San Francisco. With each glass negative wrapped first in paper, then in heavier paper, again in corrugated paper, and finally in heavy kraft paper the carefully crated collection was transported in a Bekins Moving Company van to the museum in California.

Safely delivered to the Maritime Museum the collection was unpacked, admired greatly, and housed on prepared shelves. Each negative was cleaned, rejacketed in a new sleeve, and catalogued. In an effort to collect additional information about his work methods to supplement Hester's surviving notes on his photographs, the museum enlisted the help of scores of maritime enthusiasts around the world. Those who owned his prints, letters, or business correspondence, or who could recall encounters with Hester, were generously responsive to the museum's inquiries. They provided identifications of particular ships and crews and copies of the prints they owned for study by the museum staff. This ongoing search for additional information has increased the value of the Hester collection as a reference source.

Some years later, in their house, the Sands found

Booms hoisted high off their rests, lumber sheets shackled in their bales, the swinging spar rigged on her main lower-mast, the four-mast schooner Meteor *prepares to take on her deckload. The logs afloat alongside will be stowed in her hold through her stern ports.*

an additional cache of Hester's prints, both un-mounted and mounted. These were promptly pur-chased by the University of Washington on the recommendation of Robert D. Monroe, head of the Suzzallo Library's Special Collections Department. Well into the writing of this book the Sands uncov-ered, and sent to me, a small group of personal photographs believed to be of Mr. Hester. Several are reproduced in this book.

Hester's photographs trigger a variety of reactions from those who look at them. A maritime historian, or a sailing ship enthusiast, could write one book using these photographs, enlarging on their wealth of pertinent detail with loving exactness. For an-other author these photographs might as easily sup-port a sharply focused examination of Puget Sound's deep-sea export trade in lumber and grain or they might be used to document the development of Puget Sound's port and harbor facilities. An art or photographic historian could use them to help trace the rise of artistic photography in the Pacific North-west. They form an important link as well in the general history of photography at Puget Sound. My own approach has been to examine these photo-graphs in terms of the life and day-to-day work re-quirements of a frontier photographer at Puget Sound. Not much has been written on this aspect of the history of photography on the Pacific frontier. We still know too little of how frontier photogra-phers lived, the imperatives that governed their la-bors, or the conditions that stimulated their aes-thetic responses. Additional research is badly needed to document and detail many yet unanswered questions.

Frontier photographers have largely been pre-sented till now more as symbols than as credible human beings with commonplace aspirations, strug-gling to make a meager living as their neighbors did. They are rarely drawn, as they were so often, as workmen with quite ordinary impulses plying their craft with little public recognition and even less community esteem.

The more popular posture is still to cast each of them in the guise of an artist, a conscious carrier of the great traditions of painting and drawing. Al-though there were artists among them, most frontier photographers were not. Only a handful came to photography out of previous artistic training. A per-tinent and more typical example of the manner in which many frontier photographers were trained can be seen in the life of John K. Hillers, a photographer on John Wesley Powell's Colorado River expedi-tions. He was hired originally as a handyman, to pack the expedition's supplies, pull an oar in the boats, and assist in manuevering the bulky, wet-plate cameras used by the expedition's official photogra-phers. Eager to learn he developed enormous skill in the camera's use and eventually replaced all the previous photographers. The brilliance of the photo-graphs he made in the canyons of the Colorado has rarely been equaled.

We remain uncertain still of how many frontier photographers were itinerants seeing in their cam-eras no more than an easier way of making a living than working in the forests or the mines or on farms. The life of a frontier photographer was often a mea-ger and hard one at its best. For some photography was a profession they followed throughout their lives, a career. For others, for many, photography was merely a temporary way to survive. There were some photographers who engaged in their work only to

build up a grubstake, a nest egg, looking for money they could invest to secure a comfortable future. There were those who succeeded in this path, but many failed.

For a good number of immigrants who worked as frontier photographers most any other type of business would have met their needs as satisfactorily. For many young men trying to find their way pho-tography was but one of several professions to be dabbled in simultaneously. It was one to be quickly dropped as soon as something better came along.

Hester was such a photographer. His task was learning to photograph sailing ships and their sea-men in Puget Sound's gloomy weather. He did it conscientiously and learned to make his photographs with more than commercial competence. He found the customers he needed as they found him. Their relations were agreeable and mutually profitable, Hester using his view camera and his sensitive re-sponses to advantage. He realized his goal, to make enough money to stop taking photographs in Puget Sound's distressing weather.

It is doubtful that Hester ever consciously set out to make artistic photographs. No definite record exists of his membership in any photographic society nor does any surviving correspondence indicate his interest in aesthetic matters. For him photography was all business. And yet his work amounts to far more than a mere record of Puget Sound shipping and seamen. It reveals the profound sensitivity and clear vision of an artist. We are enriched as were his contemporaries by the vivid products of his com-mercial labors.

It is a fortunate blessing his photographs have survived.

*Wilhelm Hester, circa 1915, proud owner of a spanking
new touring car, on one of Seattle's many planked roads.*

*Wilhelm Hester, 1893. The newly arrived immigrant poses
for a photograph to reassure the folks back home.*

The Photographer

During the late 1890s and the early 1900s Wilhelm Hester documented the sailing ships and the men of the Pacific Northwest export trade in grain and lumber. Centered in Tacoma the shipment of grain attracted a steady procession of sailing ships and steamers, while the huge volume of lumber requiring sea transport drew numerous vessels to Puget Sound's sawmills.

Hester's work consisted of taking and selling photographs of these ships and sailors at the Tacoma, Seattle, and Port Blakely waterfronts, the latter the location of one of the largest sawmills on Puget Sound. He was forced, most of the time, to make his pictures under difficult weather conditions, using heavy and awkward equipment. Nonetheless he produced an unparalleled photographic record of the men and sailing ships of his day. Although largely documentary in character the photographs reveal his extraordinary sensitivity to the beauty of ships and the sea.

This documentary record of Hester's is, of course, not the entire story of these men, those ships, and that trade. It could not be—but it is a technical and human document, composed of details and images, forgotten trivia and lost impressions that cannot be duplicated in traditional archival material. The pictures that Hester made are unique; no other source can provide such information. In the way that one person's impressions of one subject over a prolonged period are complete—in that way Wilhelm Hester's pictures are complete. The collection that remains of his work is historically invaluable, artistically significant, and completely unique in specific areas.

When Hester took up photography in 1893, the medium was over fifty years old. But the impact of its discovery was still being felt. We might find it absurd, surrounded as we are by photographs of our every waking hour, to consider living successfully today without their verifying reassurance at every hand. Perhaps it would prove more difficult than we are prepared to admit. Yet such a poverty of credible images faced everyone who lived in the first forty years of the nineteenth century. In their efforts to communicate with one another in those days most people were limited to reading, writing, and speech, and what little they could see and experience for themselves firsthand. Painting, its allied arts, and the crude newspaper and book illustrations then in vogue helped but little.

The discovery of photography in 1839 ushered in a visual revolution. It created new conventions for seeing, enlarging popular knowledge of the nineteenth-century world and exposing to view much that had been previously unseen and unknown. Overnight, it expanded people's images of themselves, their neighbors, their country, and their environment.

The announcement of its discovery in France was hailed with delight. At last a chemical-optical process had been found that could permanently fix an image formed by a lens and the natural light of the sun. Known as daguerreotypes to honor one of its two discoverers, a Monsieur J. L. M. Daguerre, the new process opened a hidden world to public view and at the same time ushered in a new business: taking photographs. It proved to be more than a short-lived fad. Virtually everything a photographer could point a lens at proved to be a salable subject.

In a short time, literally millions of daguerreotypes, ambrotypes, tintypes, calotypes, paper negatives, and paper prints of various kinds were circulated.

The new found enthusiasm for photography rushed on in a mounting tide creating devotees everywhere. Photographers organized themselves into clubs, associations, and even into international societies competing with one another for awards of artistic merit. Manufacturers of supplies and equipment flourished. Successful businesses to support and expand the new skills were established in most large cities of the world. Amateur photographers multiplied like locusts and in a brief time the ubiquitous family album filled with their work, the famous *cartes de visite*, were found in many homes.

In the midst of this frantic scene was the professional photographer, often quickly and poorly trained, ignorant of business, and frequently tucked away in some forgotten corner of the world. Restricted by the mechanical and optical limitations of their early-day equipment, these professional photographers did not attempt to create manipulated photographs or trick photography of the kind we are accustomed to seeing so often in our own time. Not only was it nearly impossible technically, but the hold on the imagination of the "straight view" was so strong that any image markedly different was unlikely to find many paying customers. We look in vain for candid photographs of that day. These were completely beyond their powers.

Limiting themselves to faithful views and portraits the early-day photographers produced an immense and popular visual record of their particular time

Port Blakely's sawmill embraced a noisy world of screaming saws, hissing steam, tall-sparred sailing ships, and taller green trees. From the south shore, across massed log booms in the bay, everything was mirrored accurately but the gull's screech and the hoarse grunts of laboring sailors and longshoremen.

and place. It is hardly surprising that under such circumstances so many images of people, places, and events that might be considered unimportant and commonplace were made by nineteenth-century photographers. These ordinary images are becoming increasingly valuable today to historians, researchers, archivists, and writers as evidence. They are providing detailed information that has long eluded us in our studies of the writings and paintings produced at the same time.

Until a short time ago the only well-known nineteenth-century photographer was Mathew B. Brady, recognized almost exclusively for his Civil War photographs and portraits. That situation has changed sharply. Many of Brady's equally important coworkers, and other deserving photographers of that time, are beginning to receive recognition and esteem. In the United States more serious attention is now being paid to the photographs of Robert Vance, Albert Southworth, Fred Coombes, Victor Prevost, John Plumbe, Alexander Gardner, Timothy H. O'Sullivan, A. J. Russell, Alfred Hart, Charles Savage, Jack Hillers, William H. Jackson, William S. Soule, Henry G. Peabody, Adam Clark Vroman, Emma Freeman, Frances Johnston, A. C. Forbes, Darius and Tabitha Kinsey, Carleton E. Watkins, Ben Wittick, Layton Huffman, Frank J. Haynes, David Barry, the Curtis brothers, Edward Sherriff and Ashael, to list only a very few.

Many photographers came to the U.S. from foreign lands. Such was the case with Wilhelm Hester. For thirty-odd years after the Civil War, European immigrants flocked to these shores as though gold were being given away free. The Pacific Northwest, with growing industries needing low-priced, unskilled labor, was host to its share of hopeful new

arrivals. Jobs in the forests and the sawmills were plentiful. The work was tough and grueling. It offered good food, "enough and plenty" it was called in those days. The pay was agreeable enough and opportunity for a hard worker seemed unlimited. More than one young foreign-born seaman jumped off his ship or paid his way off her to come ashore and labor in this new land.

For many Europeans, particularly Scandinavians, there was special comfort in the sights and sounds of Puget Sound. The visual similarity between this heavily timbered, wet meeting ground of the sea and the forest and their own homelands was considerable. The feeling of familiarity it provided was often reassuring to lonely immigrants. But learning to live in the new land had its hazards. Most immigrants worried about steering clear of trouble, which to them meant the law. Fearful of all officialdom, regardless of the language they spoke, they quickly learned to be wary. Being close-mouthed in general was the safest posture most of the time. The old world had taught *that* lesson of survival against tyranny to many of them.

Probing questions about any person's life history were discouraged among the immigrants. Busybodies were severely frowned upon. Well-kept personal secrets such as: Who are you?, Where do you come from?, How old are you?, were asked infrequently and answered even less. Such information, if recorded at all, was safeguarded in the flyleaf of one's family or personal Bible. These are some of the reasons we know too little about Wilhelm Hester.

Hester was born in Germany, possibly at Oldenburg, near Bremerhaven on the Hunte River on 13 October 1872. Ernst and Anna Schoening Hes-

ter, his parents, named him Wilhelm, calling him Willi throughout his childhood. It was a name used during the rest of his life by a select few intimates. He was the youngest of three children, with a sister and an older brother Ernst, named after their father.

Both young men left their North German home together, arriving on the east coast of the United States in 1890, when Willi was eighteen years old. They journeyed quickly to the west staying somewhere in Montana for three years. This period remains a blank. We know nothing of where they lived, what occupied their time, or what they learned during the years 1890–93. In the fall of 1893 the two Hesters arrived in the Northwest settling in Seattle.

Precisely when the two brothers took up photography remains unclear. Ernst Hester advertised in an 1893 Seattle business directory as a photographer, while twenty-one-year-old Willi, at the same time, appears in a different directory at a different address as an artist. The word "artist" when applied to a frontier photographer can be misleading. Many early photographers had started their careers as painters and could, if required, produce salable portraits or agreeably tinted photographs. It was not uncommon for photographers operating on the fringes of civilization to give themselves such alluring and deceptive titles as "artist" or "professor" whether they merited them or not. These titles often proved effective come-ons for unsophisticated customers. It was doubtless a common affectation among photographers in Seattle at that time.

Willi's surviving account books for the first years of his work evidence that, regardless of a number of conflicting entries in local business directories,

he was busy photographing Puget Sound shipping steadily for the five-year period 1893–98.

The year 1898, which saw the Alaskan gold discoveries widely publicized, changed many lives in the Pacific Northwest. The announcement generated a get-rich-quick mentality that raced through Seattle leaving few untouched. Even though experienced goldseekers knew they could make their "pile" easiest selling supplies in Seattle to the inexperienced miners who thronged the docks, others had to go north themselves, including Ernst and Willi Hester. Along with a shipload of equally maddened humanity they sailed for Alaska as soon as they secured steamer passage. In frenzied Seattle even that normally prosaic task was a major effort. Willi Hester only twenty-six years old, an accomplished photographer, was as eager to see the Far North as he was to find gold.

Newspaper accounts from Alaska provide scant information about their activities and their fortunes. Brother Ernst is reported investing their joint profits from several mining ventures in a brewery which he operated himself. They appear to have cleared $75,000 in the venture in a short time. Two additional claims they owned and worked, one on Anvil and the other on Snow Creek, were reportedly worth in excess of $200,000. It is possible that Alaska's Hester Creek was named by the two Hesters themselves.

Staying only a short time, Willi Hester returned from Alaska in 1899 determined to pick up once more the threads of his former life as a commercial marine photographer on Puget Sound. He appar-

ently had little trouble. The dating of his work confirms that he was active as soon as he returned from the north.

Although he made many photographs of the ships and seamen of Puget Sound's waterfronts after 1900, it was becoming a part-time concern for him. Perhaps by itself photography could no longer support

him as Puget Sound's economic climate improved and the cost of living and doing business both rose. Perhaps he felt pressed for capital for investments to secure his old age even though he was only a twenty-eight-year-old youngster. It is clear that he wanted as much money as he could earn, for he tried other ventures. He was turning increasingly to real estate speculation as a part-time occupation, purchasing raw land and property in King and other Washington State counties. He seemed to enjoy barter, filling his time buying, selling, and slowly accumulating all manner of curious objects to be boxed and barreled and kept in his home.

When he was thirty-four years old, in 1905 or 1906, he apparently gave up professional photography altogether, at least of maritime subjects. Few of his surviving prints can be accurately dated beyond that time. There are, however, at least three photographs he could have taken *only* in 1915. Their existence poses a provoking and as yet unanswered question: When did he stop making his maritime views? At some point his other part-time interests came to occupy him exclusively.

By 1929 Wilhelm Hester was reputedly worth a quarter of a million dollars. He lost all of it in the Depression. Little daunted he fought his way back to solvency creating a second small fortune of real estate holdings valued at $30,000 by the executor of his estate. According to the instructions in his will the full proceeds from the sale of his estate were to be returned to his sister in Germany.

Wraith-like in a clearing morning mist at Commencement Bay the British four-mast bark Drumblair *exhibits the lean power of hull and rigging she needed to weather Cape Horn's brutal gales.*

In his retirement Hester lived in an old, rambling wooden house atop Capitol Hill at 730 Lakeview Boulevard in Seattle. He apparently lived out his life as a near recluse if the hearsay of his neighbors is to be believed. According to some of them, his companions were limited to occasional stray animals and a few male friends who stayed with Hester for short periods of time. As far as the records show he never married. Not a single thread of gossip suggests any sort of common-law relationship. To his closest neighbors Hester appeared a genuine eccentric largely because he filled the rooms of his home with boxed and barreled items and loose accumulations of every kind of material. They report one barrel contained fifty-eight alarm clocks and quantities of small parts. Another was filled with six birdcages, two large boxes overflowing with women's hats, wooden boxes of cups without handles, and additional boxes of goblets without stems. These were typical of his accumulations. This zeal for saving everything may be the principal reason his negatives have survived. Packed in wooden boxes they awaited whatever eventual disposition Hester had in mind. His death put an end to whatever plans he had for saving his early work and thwarted any hopes he may have had of some day expanding into the junk business in earnest.

In common with many immigrants at that time, he stubbornly mistrusted the medical profession. To put it bluntly he preferred to live without a diagnosis than to die as a consequence of getting one. He undoubtedly hastened his death at the age of seventy-seven through neglect and the lack of timely professional assistance. He needed it badly. Hemorrhaging severely from upper-gastrointestinal infec-

tion he was taken, protestingly, to the Virginia Mason Hospital, where he died at 5:10 P.M. on the evening of 25 February 1947. He was buried in the Seattle Evergreen Cemetery at ten in the morning on 1 March 1947.

His executor, Mr. Raymond C. Punette, recalls him in the last years of his life as a "medium built, thin, clean-shaven man, very stubborn, somewhat parsimonious, and a collector of everything to the point of pathological obsession."

It might have been an easier life for Hester had he been a workman of the day, laboring on the ships or in the sawmills he frequented. He had not chosen an easy profession, marine photographer. The Puget Sound area in the 1890s was a virtual frontier and most small businesses struggled to find solid footing. Photography in a frontier lumber town in the 1890s was a far cry, in all of its aspects, from the well-organized operation we see about us today. Everything one needed was in short and uncertain supply, customers as well as materials. The portrait photographer had to have social and business contacts not readily achieved by a newcomer without capital. Developing a steadily salable specialty was a requirement for any business in so isolated an area and for a photographer it was an absolute must.

Even with a well established speciality, a photographer's life was difficult. The problems of getting around tree-crowded Puget Sound were many and time consuming. They made it almost impossible to conduct a profitable operation. Few photographers were equipped or trained to do everything themselves; even if they were there were not enough

hours in the day to get it all done. Traveling to see and "sell" his customers and make the necessary photographs consumed much of a photographer's time. Searching endlessly for work to keep his struggling business alive, Hester was required to drive, sail, and steamboat his way around Seattle, Port Blakely, and Tacoma day in and day out—in the gray fog, damp, cold, snow, sleet, and the now-and-again sunshine.

Hester may have simply fallen into his specialty by chance or his choice may have been a definite one among limited options. Strong circumstantial evidence exists to support the latter notion. In his time several groups of German immigrants established small communities near Tacoma. Although they were a mere handful, the settlers built fraternal and social organizations, published several German-language newspapers, and offered any homesick German immigrant that cared to visit with them a touch of the old country life and the mother tongue for reassurance. Most German immigrants in the Puget Sound area supported these tiny settlements and it would be strange if the young Hesters, uncertain and lonely in their adopted land, failed in their first years at Seattle to visit their countrymen more than once.

Although no more than an educated guess, it is reasonable to suppose that shortly after his arrival in 1893 young Willi Hester might look for customers for his new photographic business in these communities. It would be surprising if the sea-weary officers and crews of visiting German ships, in port to load wheat or lumber, did not likewise visit the same small communities to pass on greetings, visit old friends, and partake of a bit of homemade sausage,

a glass of beer, or a nip of schnapps. It seems more than likely that a newly-arrived young German photographer, an agreeable sort, struggling to make a go of it in the new land might be offered the opportunity to photograph German ships, German sailors, and German officers.

What is evident is that his recognized ability to photograph the great ships and their crews so handsomely, the sensitivity of his responses to their vivid, busy world of sawmills and grain docks, his willingness to understand and fulfill the needs of their crews helped his success as a marine photographer. He correctly sensed that many seafaring men, particularly sailing ship men, still cherished their tall ships, a surviving expression of earlier times.

Sailing ship men were a proud lot however substandard their quarters, their food, and their working conditions. They were proud of their ships and proud of themselves even though they were half a world away from their loved ones most of the time. Photographs of their well-kept ships and of themselves helped keep that pride and their devotion alive. They bought such photographs in all the great seaports of the world and prized them greatly.

Hester's photographs document the work of these men with great warmth and humanity. His identification with his sailor subjects and their limited lives of hard labor is uncommon, almost totally unknown in the work of other commercial maritime photographers. His willingness to accept the clutter of a working sailing vessel in port as the normal environment for his photographs endeared him to many of his seagoing customers. Nowhere is the human dimension of the seafarer's life revealed more strikingly than in these photographs.

See his ready acceptance of the sailors' mock solemnity, the official gravity of their officers, and the casual familial grace of the shipmasters and their seagoing families. It is in his rare portraits of the small fry of the shipmaster's family that Hester reveals the true sentiment of the artist fully at ease with himself and his subject. His image of the son of the Balmoral's master shown above is a touching image, sweet proof of Hester's tenderest responses. The informal posing of Captain Edward Gates-James and his wife on page 124 speaks to the same point, as does the affecting natural manner in which Captain Alex Teschner of the German bark *Pera*, dressed in his homemade oilskin coat, faces Hester's

camera on a wet Puget Sound morning (page 115). Frequently departing from formal, classic arrangements, he photographed the sailors in amusing groups of their own choosing or busy with ship's work aboard their own vessels awaiting their cargoes. The only photographs available of ship's crews skylarking in innocent good humor, reveling in their own shipboard high jinks, are those taken by Hester. We can share their amusement in his photograph on page 121 of the *Flottbek* gang on their own main deck surrounded by a gin-drinking steward and their own fiddle-playing bosun. Such spontaneous informality rarely seen in similarly posed photographs gives Hester's images special worth, a quality readily recognized and appreciated by the sailors.

Hester was not singular in choosing to photograph ships and sailors as a specialty. Many of the seaports of the world at the same time supported professional marine photographers. T. H. Wilton at San Francisco, Nathaniel Stebbins at Boston, S. C. Gould and his son Frederick at Gravesend on the Thames, and S. M. Hood, a talented young Australian working around Sydney's vast harbor are but a few memorable examples. Certain shipmasters, amateur photographers all, took pictures successfully at sea. Captain Henry Hudson Morrison of Port Townsend and Captain Orison Beaton of Puget Sound, both tugboat masters, Captain Walter Mallet of the American bark *Guy C. Goss*, Captain Richard Woodgett of the immortal British *Cutty Sark*, and in contemporary times Captain Alan Villiers each made enduring images. Our photographic record of nineteenth and twentieth century sailing ships draws heavily on the labors and talent of these and other less well-known men and women.

The ship, the Eva Montgomery; *the personna, Captain and Mrs. Harrison, stout Britishers; the scene, their ship-board livingroom, Captain Harrison's cabin. Hanging from the skylight, a birdcage caps the Victorian splendor of the scene. We are assured it is a ship's cabin by the braided stays securing the silk-shaded lamp overhead from swinging with the motion of the ship.*

How did Hester pursue his calling? Let us follow him as he worked his way through a normal day's activities. His working grounds were the docks and wharves of Seattle and Tacoma and the waters of Elliott Bay and Commencement Bay. Perhaps most important to him was the tiny bay at Port Blakely, directly across from Seattle. Located in that deep bay were the great seven-day-a-week sawmills of the Port Blakely Mill Company. Close by the mill was the shipyard where the Halls built their famous schooners from freshly sawn lumber.

Armed with published lists of newly arrived vessels at Puget Sound and anticipating the possibility of meeting seagoing friends again Hester traveled the Sound boarding as many ships, barks, barkentines, and schooners as he could in one day. He quickly made appointments to return and photograph them, sometimes making the views along the way as time and weather permitted. His subjects were the crews and vessels of every nationality that thronged the Sound ports at anchor or tied up at the wharves. American, British, German, French, Danish, Swedish, or Norwegian, he sought them all. On the always interesting ferry run across from Seattle to Port Blakely or south to Tacoma's Commencement Bay he could verify the anchorages of the new arrivals, planning vantage points from which he might best photograph them later on. The brief trip on these Sound steamers would provide opportunity for checking on ships up for repair in the Dockton dry-dock on Vashon Island as well as catching up on the maritime gossip of the day with his friends among the ferry crews. Although, he needed every customer he could get, in his business it was prudent to be careful to whom he extended credit.

We can almost see him carrying his 8″ × 10″ view camera firmly fastened to a heavy, ruggedly built wooden tripod, a leather case holding glass dry plates and wooden plate holders, flash powder, and his contemporary version of a flash gun. Carrying his wide-angle lenses in a separate wooden box, order pad in his pocket, a morning newspaper for the newly arrived shipmaster in his hand, he would arrive on a ship's main deck ready for business. Arrangements with the captain were made for shooting the required sittings once the brief amenities were disposed of. If the weather allowed, the views on deck would be taken first. Forbidding weather, common enough on Puget Sound, afforded Hester opportunity to photograph below in the master's cabin or saloon—an almost unheard of accomplishment among commercial marine photographers of his time. Thus in the Hester collection is found the only significant, and by far the best, record yet uncovered of the quarters of sailing ships masters, complete with the trifling mementos of their shoreside life lovingly arranged in view of the camera.

Commonplace as the subject seems to us today there are *no other known collections of maritime photographs anywhere in the world* that include more than a scant few, poorly lit, badly photographed views of a shipmaster's quarters, almost all of them taken by amateurs. In the Hester collection, however, one can see in rich detail example after example of the cabins of well-known and lesser known vessels. They range from the austere saloon of a poorly outfitted Chilean bark used by the master and a select group of his card playing, drinking companions to the richly carpeted and ornately decorated home afloat of the Master Edward Gates-James of the famous London "flyer," the four-mast

bark Lynton. Richly evocative, perhaps more so because of the dimly lit corners of the cabin, these photographs bring to life once more the feel, smell, and sense of Victorian velour, plush, satin, and leather. The varieties in taste in Victorian decoration, the styles in fashion, the mode of elegance a determined homemaker could create in a sailing ship's cabin are revealed superbly in crisp detail. Photographed either by the natural light available from the overhead skylight on the poop deck and long time exposures or assisted by the awkward flash gun and aluminum powder of those days, these unique images are proving to be important resource documents.

In a letter to the author, a British sailing ship veteran, Gavin Craig, describes such shipboard sanctuaries with feeling.

These photographs bring to life again the quiet warmth of the cabin alleyway, the comfortable low headroom and the strangeness of a carpet underfoot after the hard, wet decks outside. The diminished roar of the wind, the friendly chink of china plates on the pantry shelves and the soft click of a door hook as the ship presses down to leeward. The slow swaying of the saloon lamp, scent of fresh bread, strong tobacco, woolen blankets, kerosene oil and the recurrent gust of cold air down the companion-way from the charthouse above. And the blessed silence.

Some of the details are amusing. The decorated lamp-shade in the cabin of the Lynton. I wonder what were the colours and the material—red silk? I bet the steward had heart failure every time he lit the lamp. The plate of fruit, the reproduction of Queen Victoria and the vel-vet-framed photograph of what looks like a midwife. Probably the Master's mother-in-law.

There are no shouts of "Hey, Willie" in that ship, when the steward was required. No Sir, the little bell on the table was there for the purpose. Coal on the fire,

DIVINE, GATES & CO.,

Shipping and Custom House Agents.

TELEGRAPHIC ADDRESS:
" DIOGENES."

P.O. Box 517.

Telegrams requiring a Reply must
be prepaid.

Goods and Parcels forwarded to all
parts of the World.

11, Castle-street,

Cape Town,

14th August, 1902

Wm. Hester Esq.,

    Marine Photographer,

       Tacoma, WASH.,

         U. S. A.

Dear Sir,

      Last week I purchased from one of the crew, a
photo of the French bark "La Fontaine", taken by your firm,
and I now venture to ask you whether you can supply me with
copies of certain ships, particularly French & American,
which visit your port.   My photographer in this city, Mr.
J.Hubrich, photographs vessels in the bay and disposes of
all his copies to the crew, reserving one for myself.   I
shall therefore be very glad to know your terms per single
copy.   Should I hear from you by return of post, I shall
send you a list of thirty vessels, which are due to arrive at
your port.   If you have an photographs of vessels which
have been taken some time ago, will you be good enough to
let me know their names, as I am anxious to purchase some.

      Trusting to be favoured with an early reply,

                     I remain,

                     Yours faithfully,

C.N Vincent Solomon

P.S. Can you give me the address of photographers
in New York or Frisco, & have you a branch in S.F.

CNR

26

polish the brass fender, empty the big spittoon and clean out the birdcage.

All that and much more I see in these photographs and I thank you for the pleasure they give me.

In the master's cabin below, the formal shooting finished, Hester and the captain might negotiate for a photograph to be made of the master's much esteemed painting of his present vessel or even of his previous prized command. Rare indeed was the shipmaster's cabin that did not sport on its walls a framed photograph of his ship at anchor or painting of her under sail, gleaming in new paint, everything properly set and drawing, the ship a thing of beauty and powerful grace. It hung *always* on the after saloon bulkhead where the natural illumination from the skylight might show it off most effectively.

Produced at most seaports of the world these paintings form a valuable cross section of the several different types of ship portraiture fashionable at that time in the international maritime community. Hester's many photographs of these paintings reveal precise details of ship construction and rig and paint schemes. Such information greatly assists accurate identification of late nineteenth century sailing vessels by researchers and historians.

Photographs of these painted portraits would often be given to the ship's captain by Hester as a gift in anticipation of expected orders for additional prints. Sailors aboard the ship would dependably purchase several prints for themselves as well as their friends at home and abroad. Carried to foreign lands Hester's photographs were seen and admired by sailing ship enthusiasts. They were effective silent salesmen for Hester. He frequently received orders for his work from abroad in such letters as the one reproduced at left.

The well-known marine illustrator Anton Otto Fischer, a sailor in the British bark *Gwdyr Castle,* recalls meeting Hester in Tacoma in 1902. His book *Foc'sle Days* details the chance encounter:

One day a photographer from Seattle came aboard. He made a specialty of photographing ships coming up Puget Sound in Tacoma and Seattle harbors, and group pictures of crews. He received permission from the captain to take a picture of our crew, and we all grouped ourselves around the mainmast. Most ships had a painting of the vessel hanging in the captain's saloon, which the photographer was usually given permission to photograph. From the negative he made prints which he sold to the crew. The *Gwdyr Castle* had no such painting, much to his disappointment, but the mate told him there was a Dutchman named Bismarck in the focs'le who was always messing around with water colors. Perhaps he could paint a picture of the *Gwdyr Castle.* I was pointed out to him, and told him, sure I could make him a picture of the ship under full sail, if he could get me a sheet of water color paper, and the captain would let me have a day off.

The captain gave me the next day off, and the photographer came back the same afternoon with the paper; so the next morning I started in, standing on the settee running all around the lower bunks, with the paper propped up in my bunk, the porthole furnishing the light. I became so absorbed in my work that I didn't even take time off for the midday meal, and by evening it was finished. What the picture lacked as a work of art, it made up for in accuracy of detail and my shipmates thought it grand, an opinion in which I fully concurred. The next morning the photographer returned and was delighted too. He took the picture back to Seattle with him and returned a few days later with prints of the picture and the group photograph. He charged a dollar apiece for the prints and they went like hot cakes. Everybody including myself, bought a photograph. I even shelled out two dollars for one each, and also let the photographer keep the original.

I was so proud of my success that it never occurred to me that the photographer had used me as an easy mark. He evidently thought I was too good a thing not to be made use of further, for he took me aside and tried to convince me I didn't belong in a ship's focs'le. He wanted me to quit the ship and work for him. Why I didn't avail myself of the opportunity to settle in America, with a ready-made job, I don't know to this day, unless I wasn't yet ready to settle down, and the thought that I might settle in America hadn't occurred to me. In spite of its rigors and hardships, the life of a deepwater sailor appealed to me still. It was colorful, and I was under obligation to no one. Through it I had become hardened both physically and mentally. The photographer was very much surprised when I said no to his proposal and looking back over the years I have often wondered what would have happened to me if I had accepted and settled in Seattle in 1902.

On deck the ship's master was photographed alone on his own quarter deck. Next, in rapid succession, a photograph was taken of the captain with his strong right arm, the chief mate, and likely as not a few additional group views might be taken of the captain together with the rest of the officers. Sailors knew them, in seagoing parlance, as the afterguard. The master might then be joined with the ship's red-cheeked apprentices, if the ship carried them, for a final group photograph. Shed of their normal work clothes, tar-encrusted dungarees, and decked out in rumpled brass-bound jackets, stiff white collars slightly sea-stained, their reefer hats emblazoned with company badges, spruced up and shining, the apprentices posed with mock seriousness. Following these sittings, the "Mrs. Master," if she was aboard, joined the captain for their photograph near the after companionway or the quarterdeck skylight. Finally, if available, the master's children and the family pets were photographed together to complete the afterguard family.

From the tam-o-shantered ship's boy to the sea-booted, white-bearded "old hand" these seemingly unimpressive Norwegian seafarers symbolize the chain of sea lore mastered and shared by sailing ship veterans and novices alike.

Hester's work did not end here; the crew came next. Photos of the crew were in great demand and they proved to be a staple item for him. Mustering their sternest dignity the ship's crew, sometimes joined by their petty officers, the bos'n, sailmaker, carpenter, and donkeyman or just a few newfound shoreside friends would assemble on the main deck under the boat skids, atop the Liverpool house amidships, or on the focs'le head for their own photograph. If a local dignitary was aboard—Chaplain R. S. Stubbs of the Tacoma Seamens Institute was a frequent visitor to the sailors—he or she was invited to slip into the photographs being taken of the crew. Chaplain Stubbs seems to have accepted such an invitation more than once. One, two, or several much exposed glass plates were quickly added to the mounting pile.

Although taking photographs of a sailor's friends was strange work for most maritime photographers Hester made a number of them. The debonairly dressed group of six, four men and two women, wine glasses held high, on page 120 commands our attention. Equally vivid is the portrait of the smoldering eyed beauty and her shy friend on page 117.

Once the shooting of the ship's personnel had been completed, deck views were photographed next. Walking aft as far as he could with his view camera and tripod, stopping alongside the ship's wheel box or sometimes dead aft at her taffrail, Hester brought his wide-angle lenses into play to photograph looking forward along the vessel's decks. Hester's skill in his use of his wide angle lenses raised these "on deck" views to something approaching an art form. Superb in their crisp detail they are

treasured by those needing the information they reveal. Moving forward on the main deck with his camera he would decide on a suitable location to make a new view and turning about, looking aft, he would photograph another deck view or two. When possible he encouraged the ship's officers and her crew members to step into these unique views in natural poses. This provided a sense of personal warmth as well as a necessary measure of scale. If ship's work was going on aboard the vessel he would often take an extra shot or two, apparently for his own pleasure, maybe even hoping to sell a few prints. It speaks well of the relationships Hester enjoyed with these seafaring folk that he was welcome to make informal photographs of them at their labors.

To complete his planned day's work Hester needed to secure at least one or more classic views of the ship. It was by tradition either a broadside view at anchor or a photograph of her as she lay tied up at the wharf awaiting her cargo. These images were easily understood by the maritime community and were unfailingly popular; they were Hester's bread and butter and he produced them in abundance. Necessarily he developed his favorite vantage points from which to photograph the ships, a nearby wharf or dock, the roof of a mill, a convenient swing bridge as at Eleventh Street in Tacoma, or from Port Blakely's less crowded south shore. Even an anchored vessel near Restoration Point waiting her turn to be warped to the loading dock proved useful. Hester's varied shooting locations are tributes to his creativity. He was not easily satisfied. If the vessel he needed was moored in the stream as in Tacoma's Commencement Bay or Seattle's Elliott Bay his photographs were often taken from the deck or the

wheelhouse of a hired launch, tugboat, or barge or the decks of any anchored vessel nearby that would permit him aboard. Needless to say a firm platform and a securely braced tripod were matters of top priority in all such work. A dead flat calm was a required blessing.

Almost as popular as the many photographs he made of ships and sailors were the detailed images, both close-ups on deck and long shots, of the lumber loading process itself. He seems to have been welcome on the crowded mill docks during the hectic and dangerous work of loading as much as he was aboard the vessels themselves. The contrast between Hester, always a natty dresser, and the ill-dressed, hoarse-voiced seafarers and longshoremen that surrounded him must have been considerable. It is remarkable that Hester was able to feel adequately comfortable in those circumstances. He needed all the "cool" he could muster to create so many brilliant images of the distracting work being carried on all about him. Certainly less salable to ship's crews than his highly regarded ship portraits or group views of the men, these unusual images afford us the opportunity of studying this long-vanished process in careful detail.

Landscape photographs of Port Gamble and Blakely Bay's rugged beauty proved less popular than Hester's more widely known images of sailing ships and their crews. Nonetheless he made such views. Since his photographs were usually ordered in advance he generally avoided wasting glass plates simply for his own pleasure. He watched his pennies too closely for that kind of extravagance. Yet the landscape photographs he produced of the sawmill spits must be considered either a speculative risk Hester was willing to take or a natural response

on his part to the green splendor of the Pacific Northwest. The lack of customers for such views suggests the latter. If Hester had been able to make his photographs on color film we could see for ourselves the rich imagery that inspired him so often. Lowering gray skies, rich green trees, multicolored wood and steel vessels, sails of all shades, swirls of eddying white smoke, wheeling white winged gulls, and the mill workers homes, white on the green hillside shores, each lent their bright touches to this picture of somber beauty.

Once the picture-taking was concluded Hester would take orders for prints. As his scrawled notes testify (his handwriting was atrocious, at least when he wrote in English) the taking of these orders was often a hurried affair. On a variety of paper slips, used envelopes, and old business cards Hester jotted down, in pencil, the different orders he received and the names of the customers and the addresses all over the world to which the individual orders were to be mailed. These hastily written orders reveal some curious arrangements for payment, such as the acceptance by Hester of goods in trade, delayed payments from abroad, and collections from saloon keepers ashore. Many orders were written by sailors personally, a risky but oftentimes unavoidable arrangement for Hester.

Sailors in port rarely had cash, certainly very little at best. They were frequently allowed by shipmasters, in many cases encouraged, to purchase goods and services against wages owed them by the ship.

Ship "Cambuskenneth."

Prt Ludlow. Wash.

Nov 23rd. 1903.

Wm Hester

Dear Sir

I am sorry to state, as I feared, the man Rudert
has deserted my ship, thereby I am the entire loser of $7.50 owing to you
letting him have goods to that value.   As you know he was absent from
the ship when you went along to get the gear, and when he returned he had
already posted the things home, so that I had no security for the money.

It was much against my better judgment paying the account as I did
and I will take good care I never do such a thing again either here or
elsewhere.   Of course I cannot in any way charge this
amount to my Owners, seeing the loss they have already sustained by his
desertion, and it might be considered I had encouraged him to go by letting
him have so much.   The men tell me, you told them
they were at liberty to have what they liked, and I would pay, and they could
have the things there and then.   This was not my intention.

If you have any desire to help me out of my loss, you can remit to me C/o
Rothschild & Co. Townsend, where I hope to be during Wednesday.

All other Photographers have protected me in such matters by sowing payment until ship is ready for sea and all hands there, any defaulter accounts
always being deducted, and I hope you will do the same.   Yours Faithfully
947. C. Street. Tacoma.   Wm J. Cook.

These were due and payable at the termination of the voyage only. Many such surviving orders were written by Hester himself but countersigned by his customers. Often it was no more than a shakily drawn "OK" on the face of the order or in other cases a credible "X," the uneducated sailor's classic mark of agreement.

The master of a ship was not always able or willing to honor his sailor's commitments for many different reasons. Numerous letters in Hester's correspondence testify to the awkward nature of such arrangements for payment. The letter at left is typical.

Everything about the ordering process reveals the haste with which Hester must have worked. Moving from wharf to wharf, from ship to ship, out into the stream and back once more to yet another wharf, he spent his workday selling, shooting, and taking orders. At day's end he still needed to arrange to have his glass plates developed and printed to his instructions. Where this work was done depended upon his location when his other work was finished. He did not do it himself. As the processing he needed could only be entrusted to professionals he employed several different firms in both Seattle and Tacoma sending his work to them via Puget Sound steamers in daily transit between the two towns. When she was available, the popular steamer *Flyer* was his favorite choice, a preference he shared with many other Puget Sound residents at that time.

Hester took few photographs of Puget Sound's many steamships, photographing sailing ships almost exclusively. There are among his surviving plates, however, a hundred or more views of particular, well-known steamboats, such as the *Flyer, Chippewa*, and others. His coverage of the *Flyer* in partic-ular, including many detailed photographs of her cabins and engine room, is notable. Inasmuch as he used these steamers to transport both himself and his heavy equipment to shooting locations all around Puget Sound, it is not surprising that he would have photographed them or found new customers for his photographs among their officers and crew. The images of these steamboats on Hester's 8″ × 10″ glass plates are greatly admired by all who have seen them. Sharp, well-lit, and carefully composed they provide maritime scholars with a wealth of information.

Back and forth, morning and evening, a steady procession of Hester's negatives and prints moved across Puget Sound. The glass negatives he sent to the processing labs included carefully written instructions for developing each one, noting each exposure he had made as well as indicating the results he expected. He was a meticulous worker and very few badly focused or poorly exposed negatives are to be found among his surviving plates.

The developed negatives were quickly returned to Hester for his scrutiny and his instructions for printing from them. In this he was no less the exacting craftsman. It is rare to see any of his negative jackets today on which he has not written precise instructions for the particular exposure and any additional manipulations he wanted in his finished prints. Here is a typical instruction in his own hand written on 4 July 1904:

Schooner Clise

Make me one dozen of this schooner take the best one print them just right not so dark as the ones you send me over on the *Flyer* and a little darker than the light one. Send them over on the *Flyer* on the 4:25 trip today as I have to have them the Boat is going away.

Hester
July 4, 1904

On most negative jackets there were even more specific instructions. The number of prints needed was always included, special attention was frequently called for, and particular colors of toning were sometimes requested. Hester's daily operation was a demanding one. He was fortunate to be so energetic and determined; a different sort of person might have been unable to withstand so grueling a pace.

Most orders for Hester's photographs were for contact prints from 8″ × 10″ glass negatives, mounted individually on 10¾″ × 12¾″ heavy, gold edged cardboards embossed or printed with Hester's name and address. He also took orders for composite photographs, a type of popular image made up of the portraits of individual sailors and their officers grouped around a photograph of their ship at the center of the picture. An amusing commentary about such photographs concerns Hester's innovative method of creating them. As most sailors could not afford an individual portrait sitting Hester would carefully cut out such portraits as he wanted to use from the grouped crew photograph, paste each one into a carefully selected position on a master photograph of the ship, and rephotograph the assemblage. Prints from such a new negative were sold as composites. An additional photographic curiosity of the time was the individual bust portrait, made in the fashion described above, mounted on the face of a circular metal button that might be worn as an ornament or carried as a memento. Such portraits were made professionally for Hester and offered for sale when he visited the ships.

Once the various photographs Hester had ordered from his printers in Seattle and Tacoma were completed, mounted, and returned to him he arranged to deliver them personally to the proper customers.

If the vessel they were intended for was remaining in port he delivered the photographs to the sailors himself, payment expected on delivery. If the vessel was leaving or had departed, as was often the case, he would forward them to Port Townsend to be collected by the captain at the custom house, payment on delivery as well. Frequently Hester was obliged by his customers to serve as their private postal service, wrapping, addresing, and posting their orders to loved ones all over the world. In such cases payment, plus the expected postage, was either collected in advance by Hester or paid to him after the mailings had been completed. Many times he was obliged to request payment from a shipmaster against the wages of a sailor who had ordered his photographs, at best an uncertain way of doing business.

As already noted, Hester suffered his share of losses in such risky arrangements. In 1895 the ship *Ben Dearg* purchased a total of $84 worth of photographs and paid the bill in full only after angry letters had been exchanged. In the same year the German bark *Bertha* ran up a bill of $11.25 which was finally paid off in dunnage lumber to be resold by Mr. Hester.

A continuing question for admirers of Hester's work is why he seems to have virtually stopped photographing sailing ships after 1906. This apparently abrupt abandonment of a subject he treated with rare sensitivity remains a puzzle. The passionate character of his maritime images suggests that photographing the great ships was hardly a commonplace job for him. There is little likelihood that the ships and the sailors bored him, that making photographs of them was nothing more than a way of making a living. The answer lies elsewhere. Perhaps Hester's robust health finally failed, forcing him into less strenuous work. Perhaps he found that his business as a maritime photographer was not sufficiently steady or profitable to occupy him on a full-time basis. It may be that his other part-time interests prospered to the point of occupying him exclusively.

Although he was primarily a maritime photographer, we know that Hester accepted the same kinds of bread and butter work to supplement his income any other commercial photographer in his day would have taken as business slacked off. His curiously incomplete business records, no more than random notations, show numerous entries for photographing local picnics, baseball teams, commercial structures, hospitals, businessmen, Indians, loggers at work in the woods, and similar subjects, all ashore. Most puzzling is a small group of glass negatives of the Chinese community in turn of the century San Francisco, made apparently on speculation or for his own pleasure.

There can be little doubt that he was enterprising, scratching for every penny he could earn. His ledger entries record sales of wool, coal, old clothes, and used furniture. They suggest both the manner in which some of his customers paid for the photographs they bought from him and some of the business activities he carried on simultaneously, to make a better living.

We can only guess where he learned the skill he brought to his work as a photographer. By looking at the photographs he made, it is evident that he learned very well whatever he needed to know.

Physically slight, wiry and active, Wilhelm Hester was blessed with uncommon energy, a strong sympathy for the beauty he found in sailing ships, and an uncompromising integrity in his labors. He may never have given his own immortality a second thought as he worked in Puget Sound's transient light, braving its fog and drizzle. But he produced a collection of photographs powerful in their straightforward vision, utterly faithful to their subject, and thus faithful to their viewers as well. Little more need be asked of such photographs. Their documentary worth and aesthetic excellence are likely to ensure him a secure place in photographic history.

The Locale: Port Blakely

There were two centers to Hester's work world. One was Tacoma's wharves and wheat warehouses at Commencement Bay, the other the great sawmills at Port Blakely. While the export of eastern Washington grain was profitable the magnet that drew many of the world's sailing ships in Hester's time to Puget Sound was its lumber.

It was acknowledged by most builders that Douglas fir, the crowned monarch of the Northwest forests, was the most suitable construction timber in the world. White cedar was the finest for any sort of finishing. In Hester's time vast numbers of these trees in the Pacific Northwest were felled, sawn, and stacked on mill docks ready for loading, usually into waiting sailing ships. Each logging community, every mill spit on Puget Sound, was testimony to the energies used to transform the region's great trees into cash wealth. Lumbermen called the forests "green gold." The lumber business proved enriching for many and made towering millionaires out of a select few.

Lumbering came naturally to Puget Sound. Nowhere else in the world did Douglas fir stand taller, thicker, or cheaper to cut. Skilled laborers willing to work long hours for low pay were readily available, as were investment capital and men with experience in the lumber business. Cutting down trees as tall and as big around as Douglas firs required developing new skills. Most loggers had never seen such trees in their lives.

Sailing ships loading Puget Sound's "green gold" present a panorama of stilled beauty, surrounded by tall forests and already felled trees waiting in the bay to be sawn into lumber.

In addition, the shores of Puget Sound offered natural sites to build sailing vessels cheaply with lumber for their construction provided by sawmills no more than a stone's throw away. Experienced shipbuilders from Europe and New England, capable of designing and constructing such ships, were in good supply. There were more than enough former sailors willing to work ashore as lumbermen and mill hands. They would work as stevedores to load the ships with lumber and if necessary would go to sea once more to sail the ships to their discharging ports. Added together the lumber business at Puget Sound made profitable good sense.

It would have been God's generosity indeed if all of this largesse had been exclusive to Port Blakely alone—but it was not. There were, in fact, more profitable mill spits scattered around Puget Sound than one could visit in a week of hard touring. Included were Port Gamble, Port Ludlow, Port Madison, Port Angeles, Port Townsend, Everett, Mukilteo, Bellingham, Tacoma, and many more both great and small. This wet, wooded world of smoke, steam, drizzle, and screaming noise attracted almost every type of ship that floated.

The particular sawmill that fascinated Hester, perhaps because of its ready accessibility, was Port Blakely, eight miles across Elliott Bay, due west from Seattle. Deep inside a cool, thickly forested cove on Bainbridge Island, the loading chutes and bobbing catamarans of the Port Blakely Mill Company proved to be the pivot for a number of years for the export loading of Puget Sound lumber. There was moneymaking work at its mill docks seven days a week for any kind of vessel that could load and deliver a lumber cargo safely.

Port Blakely was justly famous, well known to the world's windjammer sailors. Among sailing ship

men it was a name that conjured warm memories. John Masefield, England's poet laureate, recalled Port Blakely in recounting the history of the four-mast bark *Wanderer*, the British sailing ship in which he served as a sailor:

The port of Blakely was then an anchorage near an island on which there was a big sawmill. The timber was towed in long rafts to one side of the island, dragged upon travellers to the saws, and thrust down hence onto shoots which led to the ship's loading ports on the other side. The ships were loading only choice logs from the first real cutting of the Washington forests. (A thirty-foot log was reckoned small.) The shore and anchorage were littered with good waste wood: logs eight feet long by four feet circumference were used as dunnage: and all ships there burned wood by day and night, and stored it for passage home. Even so, the waste of the sawmills burned day and night in two immense bonfires "as high as houses," which were fed mechanically by an endless chain. These bonfires were thronged at night by the inhabitants and visitors. . . . As ports went in those days the place was a good port, where sailors had fairly easy days and pleasant evenings. There were numerous temptations to desertion. In Seattle, across the bay, miners from Alaska would still pay for their drinks with gold dust or little nuggets. There were also many crimps in the district, who lived by the sale of men's bodies to shipmasters in need of crews.

Working seven days a week and around the clock the whining saws of Port Blakely's mills ripped great tree trunks apart into millions upon millions of board feet of lumber. Ships' crews and gangs of longshoremen worked at the loading docks unceasingly, even in Puget Sound's ever present rain, to fill the holds of the ships and pile their decks with Puget Sound's

best lumber. They crammed every stick of lumber they could into the holds, wedging it tightly against movement once the ship was underway. Sawn lumber in various sizes was always loaded through the ship's hatches on the main deck, frequently with the aid of wooden loading chutes. As the moored vessel often loomed some feet higher than the mill wharf it was necessary to get the lumber, made up into sling loads, up and onto the ship's deck. At Blakely this was accomplished by means of a series of chutes, long wooden troughs sloping upward from the mill wharf to the ships taffrail at the stern, thence forward over additional chutes, supported by timber cribbing piled high on the poop, and finally down into the open hatches. Sometimes mill-built catamarans, floating wooden structures bobbing in the water as the tide rose and fell between the ship's stern and the wharf, supported these heavy wooden chutes.

Stowing lumber took time even in the hands of skilled stevedores. At least ten days were required to lay down a lumber cargo, a stick at a time, in the hold of an average sailing vessel. Many ships did not accept a full load at Blakely, completing their loading at Tacoma, Ludlow, or the Port Angeles mills further out on the Sound.

After a ship's hold had been stowed full of all the lumber it could accept, and tightly secured, additional lumber was loaded on the main deck. Construction of this load was the responsibility of experienced longshoremen, carefully laying down one timber after another to create a compact mass. Oftentimes the load of lumber on deck towered as much as twelve to fourteen feet high. It had to be chained and secured with heavy turnbuckles for safe passage. Too often these deckloads shifting in strong weather could be fatal and to forestall such danger the massive load of lumber was lashed to itself with heavy chains, and the completed deckload then secured with additional chains and turnbuckles to the ship's sides. Even so the sound of such a mass of timber groaning against its bounds in protest, high above one's head on deck, could be disquieting once the ship was at sea.

A lumber cargo could include timbers, huge balks of wood, 24″ × 24″, at least sixty feet or more in length. In those days any log larger than 16″ × 16″ qualified as a timber. Such great logs were impossible to load through the small hatches of most ships. They were maneuvered and manhandled into the ship's lower hold through lumber ports, square openings cut into the ship at her bow and stern to allow more direct and easier access. These handy ports were used both for loading the great timbers and for discharging them at the ship's destination.

Steam donkey engines on the ships and on the wharves often provided power to help snake the timbers into place in the hold. If a vessel was moored inconveniently for loading off the mill wharf or had no donkey engine aboard, stevedores sometimes employed a donkey boiler and hoisting engine mounted on a floating barge. In this fashion steam power could be made available by towing or warping the barge alongside whatever ship required such assistance.

Vessels came and went regularly, and the endless jockeying of heavily loaded vessels into seemingly impossibly small berths remained an impressive demonstration of seafaring skill. When no berths were available, a frequent occurrence with so many ships arriving each day, the new arrivals often anchored in the bay, usually between Blakely Rocks and Restoration Point, a favorite dumping ground for the rock and sand ballast ocean-going vessels frequently carried.

Little of the great trees that could be sold was wasted. Every type and size of lumber the mill could cut found its way into ships' holds. At any time on the wharves there were pit props to shore up mine shafts in Australia and South Africa, shingles, fence posts, railroad ties, construction timbers, and great trees called "Jap squares" for the resawing mills in Japan. Anything that the remarkable Douglas fir could be used for was loaded into and onto these ships that Hester photographed at Port Blakely.

Once loaded and ready for sea the ships were towed out of Blakely harbor by one or another of the mill tugs, the little *Sarah M. Renton* or the relic of earlier days, the paddle wheel steamer *Favorite*. In the fledgling years of the mill's operations the towboat *Blakely*, a converted sailing vessel, offered her services as a towboat. Well clear of the bay, setting sail as they went, the loaded vessels were turned over to more powerful seagoing tugs for the long tow eighty sea miles northwest through Puget Sound. The way led past blustery Cape Flattery. Finally the tug and her tow entered the North Pacific where the sailing ship was whistled on her way by her departing tug.

The four corners of the waiting world were the destinations of these sailing vessels. A coastwise passage on the Pacific Coast usually meant San Francisco, San Pedro, or San Diego. Offshore, as sailors

called deepwater voyages, meant any of the ports on South America's west coast, Australia, New Zealand, Hawaii, China, or east around Cape Horn to European seaports. The ships' arrivals were eagerly awaited. Merchants and builders everywhere needed the lumber produced in the Pacific Northwest.

Almost every nation that owned or registered ships sent them to Port Blakely at one time or another. The lumber there was cheaper and better than anywhere else in the world, the sailing ships that carried it cost little to operate, and the men who manned them cost even less. For years ships came by the hundreds. Any vessel that floated and could carry sail would do nicely. Old ships or newly built ones, iron, steel, or wood, barks or schooners, it didn't matter, they came to the Blakely mill wharves to load cargoes of prime Puget Sound lumber. Powerful wooden barkentines and tiny, two-masted schooners, veteran lumber carriers of the 1860s and 70s, lay in tiers at the wharves. Side by side they crowded newer and larger vessels, wall-sided four-mast barks from Europe, slim-lined full-rigged ships, each name hallowed to windship sailors.

As Hester's photographs show, the season of the year made little difference. Any day, winter or summer, was like any other, an endless picture of changing maritime beauty. Every variety of deep-sea rig afloat came to load sweet-smelling lumber off the Port Blakely wharves. Here were proud "flyers" returning empty from the west coast of South America, deep-bellied iron and steel carriers, ships and barks under Britain's Red Duster, ships launched in the smokey Clyde shipyards, worn out timber

droghers owned by other Puget Sound sawmill companies, and handsome schooners and barkentines freshly launched at the nearby Hall Bros. shipyard. Tugging at their moorings under Puget Sound's leaden skies or alive with softly slipping shadows under a summer sun, the ships that called at Blakely were a vision of lean grace.

For hundreds of years Blakely Bay had been a lonely tree-encircled cove on the shores of Puget Sound. It was no different from many others exactly like it and only Siwash Indians felt at home there. The first European to give recognition to Bainbridge Island and Blakely Bay was a tired British explorer, Captain George Vancouver. Probing for a safe anchorage to repair the storm-damaged top hamper of his four-hundred-ton sailing ship, H.M.S. *Discovery*, Vancouver dropped anchor on 19 May 1792 at the southern tip of Bainbridge Island in thirty-eight fathoms of clear water. He was delighted to find a "cove, a small opening to the westward," encircled on both sides with tall Douglas firs. They were precisely the kind of timber his ship's carpenters needed to fashion replacement spars. Vancouver was sufficiently pleased to comment in his journal on "the small cove little worthy of further notice." He neglected to name the cove at that time, however, having more serious responsibilities. It remained for the officers of Lt. Charles Wilkes's United States Exploring Expedition to name it Port Blakely in 1842. They honored a colleague, a distinguished fellow officer, a naval hero of the War of 1812, Johnston Blakely, master of the sloop-of-war *Wasp.*

The bay remained ignored and unused for several years. In 1851 Captain William Renton, a disappointed gold-seeker, a Nova Scotian seafaring man from Pictou, arrived at Puget Sound aboard the Boston schooner *Mary and Jane*. She had come north to cut and deliver a cargo of piling and timbers for the Pacific Mail Steamship Company of San Francisco. The plentiful Bainbridge Island forests impressed Captain Renton so much that when the little schooner departed Puget Sound with her cargo, he was no longer aboard. He had decided that the dense timber stands in such close proximity to water were the stuff of his dreams. If the infant California settlements of that time were to grow, he reasoned, they would need Puget Sound's lumber. By creating a sawmill on Puget Sound's shores he could profit handsomely. So he thought.

With a partner, C. C. Terry, he established a small sawmill in 1852 at Alki Point on Elliott Bay. The mill was located in an exposed position and suffered from Puget Sound's strong winds. The partners were forced to give it up. Renton pioneered a second, larger sawmill in 1853 at Port Orchard and after a serious injury in a boiler explosion in 1857 returned a second time to San Francisco. He reappeared again on Puget Sound six years later in 1863 with a new partner, Dan Howard, selecting Blakely Bay for his third sawmilling venture. He was attracted by the bay's deep water, deep enough for ocean-going vessels. Remembering the exposed position of his first mill at Alki Point he was especially grateful for the protection against the wind afforded at Blakely Bay.

He entered a claim for a townsite he named Port Blakely on 11 July 1863. Built at a cost of $80,000 on hastily cleared land on the north shore, his new mill started cutting logs in April 1864 and was successful from the first day. Hundred-foot fir trees grew right at the water's edge and could be had for no more than the cost of labor for cutting and towing them to the nearby sawmill. The new mill's daily capacity was nearly fifty thousand board feet. Its first cargo was shipped to San Francisco aboard the wooden bark *Nahumkeag* on 22 May 1864.

As new markets for sawn lumber developed, the Port Blakely mill prospered dramatically. Renton took in a partner once more in 1868, renaming the company Renton, Smith & Company. In 1873 Billy Renton's loyal bookkeeper since 1856, Charles S. Holmes, was taken into the growing business as a junior partner, the company renamed again as Renton, Holmes and Company. In 1881, as the firm was gaining a reputation as "the largest sawmill in the world" it was renamed once more as the Port Blakely Mill Company. Its assets included capital stock of $500,000, more than eighty thousand acres of prime timberland, a fleet of wooden sailing ships, a few tugboats, and a thirty-five-mile railway from Grays Harbor country to Little Skookum Inlet near Kamilche. A log dump was established there from which the former Russian gunboat S.S. *Politofsky* towed felled logs in rafts to the Blakely mills. The railway included four locomotives and numerous boxcars and flatcars.

Disaster struck the enterprise in 1888. A fire started in a hotbox on the countershaft of the head saw. It quickly engulfed the mill, destroying the original building, a wooden structure with diamond shaped windows. While a crippling blow, it was not altogether devastating. Rebuilding commenced as soon as cooling ashes permitted and in less than five months newly turning saws were cutting logs once more.

Further crises awaited the mills. Captain Renton died in July 1891. He had been totally blind for several years. Being obliged to tap his way along the mill docks had been a hard blow for so vigorous a man. The leadership of the business passed to his two nephews, John Campbell, a longtime mill superintendent at Blakely, and his brother James. They expanded the mill facilities increasing its daily cut to 400,000 board feet of sawn lumber.

Their 1891 sawmill was an awesome accomplishment for its time. The main wooden building stretched for 438 feet. Its width was 101 feet. In front of the main mill to the east stretched wharves, storehouses, offices, and a drying house capable of handling a quarter of a million board feet of lumber. The mill was equipped with two log chutes and a variety of saws including two sets of double circular saws with renewable teeth capable of cutting nine-foot logs. There were two resaws, two sets of gang saws, two lath mills, four planers, one timber planer for large timbers, and eleven trimmers. Logs were hauled up the slipway from the log ponds by log "dogs" attached to an endless messenger chain. The mill created its own steam power and it provided electricity from its own plant. Running full tilt it could cut nearly one million board feet a day, employing 250 hands *inside* the mill and over 500 in *outside* work in the mill yards, loading wharves, log booms, and storehouses. It had the look and feel of a small successful empire. In many ways it was.

The ready availability of prime timber milled to measure made it virtually inevitable that wooden shipbuilding facilities would eventually be developed at Port Blakely. A quarter of a mile east of the mill on the bay's north shore, the Hall brothers, Winslow G., Isaac, and Henry Knox Hall, brought their heritage of New England shipbuilding skills to Puget Sound. Specializing largely in wooden sailing vessels for the lumber trade, the Halls built schooners and barkentines that filled the growing need on the Pacific Coast for fast sailing vessels to transport large lumber cargoes safely.

The Pacific Coast seafaring community regarded the vessels produced by the Hall Brothers shipyard as minor legends in their day. Easily recognized for their graceful beauty and strong construction, these ships were referred to by West Coast seamen as "Hall built," an acknowledged accolade of merit.

The Halls started shipbuilding at their Port Ludlow yard, originally near the sawmill, in 1873. Unable eventually to secure dependable quantities of the lumber they required, they moved in 1880 to Port Blakely. Captain Renton assured them that suitable lumber would always be available from his sawmill near the proposed yard location. It was a wildly successful relationship. Captain Renton faithfully kept his promise, even building, at his own expense, a set of wooden tracks shod with strap iron to carry the mill's sawn lumber the quarter mile between the sawmill and the Hall shipyard.

Sawmills dotted Puget Sound spits wherever there were trees available for cutting. Port Ludlow, shown here, was the original site of the Hall Brothers shipyard, which moved to Port Blakely in 1880 when the Ludlow mill failed to supply the prime lumber required for wooden ships.

The Halls provided steady work for shipbuilding craftsmen, investment opportunities for ship and mill owners, and an available market for shipbuilding timber. The frequent launchings of their ships provided gala social occasions for the tiny Blakely community. Offering rare relaxation these launchings attracted the entire small population free to attend them and occasionally visiting crewmen from the waiting vessels moored in the bay.

The launch in 1881 of the three-mast schooner *Maria R. Smith* witnessed the completion of the first of seventy-seven wooden ships built by the Hall Brothers at their Blakely yard. The last was completed twenty-two years later, in March 1903, as they sent the 1,260-ton five-mast schooner *George E. Billings* careening down her greased building ways into Blakely Bay. Named after a Hall son-in-law, a top-level yard executive as well, the schooner was the largest built at Port Blakely. Shortly afterwards the old Blakely yard was sold to James Griffith & Co., which moved it to Winslow, a town on the north side of Eagle Harbor, named for Winslow Hall.

Alan H. McDonald, who came to Port Blakely in 1891 as an infant and was employed in the Hall Brothers yard as a twelve-year-old, recalls in an article he wrote for the Puget Sound Maritime Historical Society journal, *The Sea Chest*, of June 1971:

I was about 12 when I went to work in the Hall Brothers shipyard as a messenger boy and doing things like boiling pitch for caulkers and installing pine deck plugs. I worked after school hours at the yard and also sold newspa-

pers. . . . Hall Brothers yard was about a quarter of a mile from the Port Blakely mill. The company had moved there from Port Ludlow because of wanting to be near a mill and this town has the biggest one anywhere around.

The shipyard had a line of rails and a little four-wheeled horse drawn cart by which to pull lumber from the mill down to where building was going on. The best ship lumber was cut from trees in winter when the sap was down. It lasted longer than planks cut in other seasons.

When I began at Port Blakely all of Hall Brothers' work was construction of sailing vessels. They would build three at a time. They had no cranes, but carried all the lumber by hand.

In putting hulls together they used treenails, round pegs made of oak an inch and a quarter in diameter. These were brought from the East. Our pine pitch for the seams on deck came from the Carolinas. All the boring of holes and driving of treenails was done by hand. The men who did this were called fasteners instead of carpenters and got a different rate of pay.

The sails, rigging, wire rope, hoops, castings and donkey boilers were bought from San Francisco. The Blakely store carried all kinds of goods and outfitted the ships. It was a big business, with a warehouse where flour and supplies like that were stored in carload lots. The mill company owned the store.

By 1891, Captain George Vancouver's "small cove" stretching east and west into Bainbridge Island housed an impressive sawmill community. Although a mill company town, and tiny by contemporary standards, it was a model of its kind on Puget Sound.

Lying some eight miles west from Seattle, the Blakely community then depended completely, as the residents of Bainbridge Island still do today, on ferry service for communication with the Washington mainland to the east. Originally served by

the mill company's tiny steamer *Sarah M. Renton*, Bainbridge Island in 1891 relied on the steamer *Michigan*, which made the eight-mile run twice daily in about three quarters of an hour or less.

The population at Blakely in 1891 was about 1,500 souls, its largest ever. The seventy-five room Bainbridge Hotel, the community's stellar tourist attraction completed in 1873, still stood although little used. Everything at Port Blakely was on company-owned land and it all looked very much alike as a consequence. At the head of the bay, a mile and a half west from its mouth, stood the rebuilt mill, forty or more single men's cottages, and five double cottages for visiting shipmasters and their families dubbed the Honeymoon Houses. Scattered over the base of the north shore, shadowed by the encircling hill, were fourteen double houses for married couples and approximately seventy-five singles for mill employees. All were built of wood to a similar plan and painted white. Even the wooden church with its white steeple contributed to the unmistakable New England look at Port Blakely. Across the bay on its south shore, the original location for the homes of the Siwash Indians and later a colony of Japanese settlers, stood a planing mill, a telephone pole cross-arm factory, and a number of small businesses including a small hotel and several saloons. It was known as Walville.

46

Even though Port Blakely was a small village, life there was far from grim or dull. Evelyn Ward McDonald, a child of pioneer settlers, described the life she remembered in an article printed in the September 1972 issue of *The Sea Chest,* the journal of the Puget Sound Maritime Historical Society:

The mill ran night and day, the huge burner and twin slab fires threw up cinders and dust that sprayed the whole countryside not to mention the intense heat and flickering blaze that could be seen for miles. The acrid odor of newly sawed lumber could be detected miles before the town came in sight. Some mill workers bought small farms and walked back and forth to work morning and evening.

Single men earned about $26 per month, plus room and board, and though married men earned more there was little left after paying for food and clothes at the company store.

That company store was a compilation of goods so diverse and so complex as to defy description. They served customers from a half dozen nations. Barrels of salt fish for the Scandinavians, rice and strange-sounding food stuff for the Orientals some wrapped in straw matting, kegs of salmon bellies in brine plus barrels of salt pork and beef for outgoing vessels.

One whole side of the store was stacked with ready made clothes for men, most of it for cold and rainy weather. Heavy underclothing, oilskins sou'westers and gumboots supplied sailors as well as their shore-side fellow workers. Women's clothes were not placed on display but more often stashed away in deep drawers, but yard goods were stacked to the ceiling. Every woman made the clothes for her family. Often brightly colored-sprigged material went aboard ships for trade in foreign ports.

The cookhouse, operated by the mill, and for the single men was run by the Chinese workers. They turned out good plain food and plenty of it. The Chinese made up a small minority of the town's population and were seldom in trouble. Only when a ship arrived with a Chinese cook or cabin boy did one see them about with their long pigtails and black cloth pants and jackets. They lived close to the cookhouse or the main hotel built near the center of town.

The social life of Port Blakey was rather evenly divided between the schools, the churches and the lodges. An elementary school on the hill above the town prepared students for Seattle high schools or boarding school at a more distant town. Church and Sunday School services of different denominations were often held in the town's larger homes until a church of their choosing could be built. A large hall took care of all lodge meetings as well as social affairs for the community.

Port Blakely had telegraph connections with Seattle as early as 1874 through a cable laid from Restoration Point to Alki. The first local mail delivery was provided by wheelbarrow by a Mr. Benner in 1896. Harry Price served as postmaster and telegrapher during these years.

Dr. C. C. Kellam was the town's only doctor providing excellent care and emergency surgery. Families for miles around cherished the sight of his horse and buggy as he made his rounds, whether it be on an errand of mercy or an exchange of his ready wit.

Many at the time thought that this incredible empire of sawmills, sawdust, and sailing ships on Puget Sound might never crumble, but eventually it did. Its end was neither sudden nor dramatic. As the lumber industry gradually became modernized, improved technology inexorably required new ways of doing business. It was sink or swim. If the lumber companies, always fiercely competitive, were to survive, they had to reduce overhead costs and take advantage of new methods of production.

As Puget Sound greeted the turn of the century it was clear that the Port Blakely Mill Company, still a dizzyingly busy operation, had seen its best days. A brief period of ownership by David E. Skinner and John Eddy changed little. Much more than sheer optimism was required, for the sawmilling business was becoming modernized with great speed. Innovations in lumber processing allowed sawmilling to be carried on closer to the felling point in the dark forests. Tractors and powerful donkey engines replaced old-fashioned ox teams, the bullwhacker of legend, and the greased skid road in the forest floor. Chain saws were more effective than double-bitted axes and they required even fewer loggers than the old days.

Steamships, in ever greater numbers, competed with sailing ships for lumber cargoes. The "tin pots" were more dependable, carried greater loads, and being faster than sailing ships could make more trips. Lumber from the mills shipped coastwise was soon loaded onto barges towed by steamers and eventually was hauled by motor truck. These improved methods of transport drove old-fashioned sailing ships from the lumber trade completely.

Another enemy of the old sawmills was fire. Many of them burned more than once and few remain standing today. Substantial vestiges of only one important mill, Pope and Talbot's sawmilling enterprise at Port Gamble, can still be seen much as it was in the days of its operation.

There was no way to beat or ignore such challenges except to keep up with the changes. As the lumber industry substituted new methods for old, instituting even more drastic changes in their sawmilling operations, adapting their sales efforts to the innovative marketing techniques used by competitors, the preeminence of such old-fashioned mill spits as Port Blakely diminished and eventually passed away completely.

The Hall Brothers saw what was happening. They moved fast, selling their Blakely yard in 1903. The mill burned again in 1907 and was rebuilt to half its size. It was dismantled once and for all in September 1914. Like many of the once-prosperous mill spits, Port Blakely died a lingering death. The utility companies moved out first and then in quick succession the power company, the telephone company, the ferry to Seattle, and finally the tiny post office. Within a matter of months the formerly prosperous sawmill community had become a ghost town.

Port Blakely is totally gone today. No evidence is left of the mills, the wharves, the houses, the stores, the bandsaws that could trim a log forty-eight inches square. All that remains is a bit of concrete and a few rotten stumps at low tide. They alone recall the colossus that once flourished at the head of Blakely's now quiet bay.

Gordon Jones wrote movingly of Port Blakely's passing in an article published in the March 1961 issue of *Motor Boating:*

For many years Port Blakely has been a "ghost" settlement. It is no longer a port; it is a phantom, a ghost of its former self. Gone are the ships, the sailors, the roughnecks, the saloons, the gilded ladies. The sweet-smelling, long-fibered straight grained fir is no longer loaded through the bow ports of down east medium-clippers and port painted limejuicers; or trundled over the sterns of eager fore-and-afters, anxious to load and get away for southern coastal ports, or Australia or the Fiji Islands. Gone, too, are the mills, wharves with their stacks of lumber ready for shipment, the cottages of the millhands, the shacks of Japtown across the bay, the Indian village, the shipyard, the caulker's mallets and even the crackle of the continually burning slab pile. All have faded into stillness.

The water in the cove is cool and quiet now. Blakely Bay is as still and calm as it used to be before lumbering began. Once again it is shadowed by dense forest, the newly-grown trees standing in green splendor as they once did. Only Hester's photographs are left to recall the activity and excitement of the Blakely mill, the crowded docks, and the tall ships that took on cargo there. With his 8" × 10" view camera, his artistry, and the integrity of his vision, Hester captured the charged beauty of that lonely sawmill spit forever.

Page 50: The newly arrived five-mast schooner Snow & Burgess, *formerly a Maine-built wooden full-rigged ship, a Downeaster, is kedged into her loading berth helped by a capstan floating alongside amidst the log boom.*

Page 51: Taking on a hold full of Puget Sound "prime" for southern California delivery the well-kept four-mast topmast schooner Wempe Bros. *adds graceful beauty to Blakely's rugged north shore.*

Staggering to sea under a fourteen-foot deckload of timber, the four-mast barkentine William Carson (the white ship at center left) sailed from Port Blakely for Sydney on 1 August 1899. Only five months later, on 27 December in the Oahu Channel, she was lost in collision with the Hawaiian interisland steamer Claudine, her captain and crew safely rescued.

Below: Such sidewheel tugboats no longer churn the deep waters of Blakely Bay. Manueverable, tough, and powerful, this aptly named mill tug, the Favorite, proved herself a darling to ships that needed her agility and stubborn strength.

Left: With her hold full of lumber securely wedged against movement, the crew of the four-mast bark Tinto Hill begins construction of her deckload. Sling loads of lumber are drawn up the wooden chutes angling up from the wharf deck to her stern, over her taffrail, and onto her decks. Without the steam power of the donkey engine, floating on a barge alongside, the job would take forever.

Right: Leaning against the wooden railing surrounding the well left in the deckload by longshoremen to provide access to the ship's pumps, this sea captain, pipe in hand, appears confident and ready for sea. With some irritation he asks, "Where's the tug?"

Left: Ships' masts and spars almost blot out the cloud-filled horizon at Blakely, as the crew of the British four-mast bark Ancyra pause from their exhausting work at the request of Hester, the photographer.

Right: Mirror-smooth lumber chutes made the task of getting heavy lumber off the wharf and onto the ship's deck a practical possibility. Without hauling power provided by a handy donkey engine even the helpful wooden chutes mattered little.

Left: Hester's appearance, with his camera and tripod, on the Blakely wharves provided a welcome break for weary longshoremen and seamen. No matter which ship or crew he was preparing to photograph, whoever was able, nearby, edged into the scene.

Right: Once off the wharf, on board the ship, lumber was moved forward or aft over additional chutes to an appropriate hatch for loading in the cavernous hold or as part of a deckload being built.

Page 60: Shielded partially from Puget Sound's drizzle by canvas tarpaulins the working crew of the German ship Parchim create a typical Hester portrait, a model of casual posing.

Page 61: Standing wherever they can on the cluttered decks of the ship Lancing, a converted French steamer, the Norwegian crew, officers, cooks, stewards, and the ship's dog lend their presence to the frenzied scene at the Blakely docks. Bolts of waste lumber in the foreground can feed the donkey boiler or as stout chocks can help wedge the deckload securely against shifting underway.

Only minutes away from launch in 1901 the five-mast lumber schooner H. K. Hall, *named for one of her builders, looms over her admirers, assorted yard workers and invited guests assembling for the gala event.*

Right: Her freshly caulked deck planking still unscraped the five-mast schooner H. K. Hall, *decorated with flags, awaits release into Blakely's deep water. For this special occasion, her white-bearded builder is joined by his workmen and friends.*

Page 64: Three Hall Brothers beauties in different stages of construction, the lumber schooners Wm. H. Smith, Winslow, *and* Lottie Bennett, *grace the yard's building ways in 1899.*

Page 65: Tree trunks for use as pilings were shipped along the Pacific Coast in wooden cradles called log booms. Built of the heavy timbers shown here and towed by steamers or powerful tugboats, cradles were filled with logs and chained and turnbuckled into a rigid mass. Although this was a novel idea, it never proved sufficiently practical to pay its own way.

The Locale: Tacoma

Sailing ships calling at Tacoma at the turn of the century for grain cargoes provided Hester with many opportunities to ply his trade. In his time Washington State looked to its abundant grain harvests for much of its prosperity. Coastwise and deep-sea shipping were dominant factors in the expansion of the state's overseas commerce; lumber and grain were its day-to-day staples.

Puget Sound was particularly well-suited to the needs of sea-borne transport. A small triangle formed by Tacoma to the south, Seattle thirty miles north, and Port Blakely on Bainbridge Island eight miles directly west across Elliott Bay from Seattle formed the center of this activity. It was Wilhelm Hester's work world.

By Hester's day sailing ships had fallen upon hard times. Their glory days were finished. The competitive pressures of steamships, faster, more dependable, and capable of carrying larger loads, had reduced the number of available sailing ship cargoes to a precious few. Those remaining were often only marginally profitable.

Puget Sound with its many cargoes of lumber and grain proved to be one of the last refuges of the world's dwindling fleet of windjammers. Ships discharging in San Francisco often found it prudent to sail in ballast, with empty holds, to Puget Sound in search of work. It was hard to wait, month after

Tacoma's City Waterway dredged from a twelve-acre mud-flat provided deepwater wharfage for a long line of loading ships moored bow to stern. The grain they took as cargo was stored in this immense complex of wooden warehouses lining the wharves in solemn procession.

month in Richardson's Bay, for a grain cargo interminably slow arriving from California's central valley. Eastern Washington grain required sea shipment and sailing ships were cheap carriers. Many shipmasters found it more profitable to lift an available grain cargo in Tacoma than to swing on an anchor in Sausalito.

Tacoma had not always been able to offer grain cargoes off her wharves. In the beginning, shortly after the Civil War, it was a disastrously different situation. Tacoma had been a slow starting community, originally named Commencement City in 1869 by its founder, General Matthew Morton MacCarver. At the outset it was little more than a muddy frontier village located where the Puyallup River, flowing west off Mt. Rainier's flanks, joined the Sound forming Commencement Bay in the process. Huddling under the peninsula's south shore bluffs it gave little indication in its formative years of its bright future. It had only the immense natural anchorage of Commencement Bay itself, bounded by Brown's Point to the north and Point Defiance to the south. Tacomans correctly sensed that this well-sheltered bay could be the key to their future success if a port with suitable wharves could be built to support the ships that might come there. Much hard work lay ahead of the realization of their dreams.

They literally started from scratch, for everything required to construct a functioning port had to be built from the bottom up. The twelve-mile estuarial tideflat at the head of Commencement Bay was an impossible location to develop a seaport. The only sensible site was the foreshore under the bluffs

where primitive but serviceable wharfage slowly replaced the original settlers' muddy landings. Shabby wooden shacks followed, and proper wooden homes in random disorder soon struggled up the sloping hills stretching west to Point Defiance. The business section clustered around Pacific Avenue while under the low hills the original village, Old Town, carried on in bawdy squalor. In the early 1870s Tacoma seemed destined for little more than muddy mediocrity.

The railroads expanding into the Pacific Northwest at that time, the Northern Pacific, the Great Northern, and Oswald Villard's Oregon Railway and Navigation Company, building along the Columbia River's south bank to Portland, proved to be Tacoma's salvation. They were the key to transforming Tacoma into a major seaport.

Once the Northern Pacific decided on Tacoma over Seattle as its Pacific Coast terminus and western headquarters, the die was cast for Tacoma. In their zeal the Tacomans had given the railway speculators more free land than any other village bidding for the terminal location. It was worth it in the long run, for it proved to be the shot in the arm Tacoma had been looking for all along.

The Northern Pacific's first train arrived in Tacoma on 16 December 1873. It took nearly a month more before railway service opened officially. On 5 January 1874 through service from Kalama on the Columbia River to Tacoma was initiated. The railway had arrived at last.

Commercial and residential growth immediately accelerated. Within months a complex of railway shops had been built on six hundred of Tacoma's freshly cleared acres. Most importantly the railway's

This portrait of the lean decks of the British four-mast bark Clan Galbraith, *a study in sailing ship detail, emphasizes the length of the Northwestern warehouse, "the longest grain storage facility in the world." Tacomans considered this a hard fact rather than a boast.*

arrival created new opportunities for successful shipment of grain to Tacoma by rail. The network of tracks feeding into the Northern Pacific's main line allowed Eastern Washington grain farmers to ship their sacked wheat *directly* to Tacoma's wharves for transhipment rather than farther south to Portland as they had been doing customarily. It was the crucial step all Tacoma had dreamed about from the beginning, the assistance they knew they had always needed.

As rail arrangements at Tacoma's port were strengthened the advantages of its commodious anchorage took on increased importance in financial circles. Its well-sheltered harbor encouraged shippers and financiers to look again at its seaport potential. But in spite of the increased enthusiasm on all sides the port's value to Portland's grain shippers remained to be proven in practice. Tacomans needed grain shipments to make their point.

Portland, on the Willamette River to the south, in Oregon Territory, had been for years *the* recognized grain shipping center in the Northwest. Serious competition from Tacoma had always seemed impossible and Portlanders hooted at the idea whenever it was discussed. Sailing ships were easily available at Portland for charter. Wharves, warehousing, and mill facilities were abundant and in addition several large flour mills flourished on the river close to the loading wharves. But grain shippers in the Pacific Northwest were eager for a second grain port on the coast. Portland had proven to be a mixed blessing.

Towing and pilotage charges normally high on the river were much higher at Portland. It was believed they were administered by a virtual monopoly at Astoria. Shippers and shipmasters alike hated the dangerous Columbia River bar at its mouth at Astoria. The 112 miles of shoal-cluttered channel upriver to Portland added little to its attractiveness. Its several disadvantages were both hazardous and costly. Such improvements as federally financed jetties at the Columbia River mouth and additional dredging of the river were still far in the future at that time.

Tacomans were confident that they could handle the flood of grain they expected to come to their port over the new rail lines. They were itching for their first test cargo. When it came it was far from the flood expected. It was only the merest trickle.

Tacoma's first wheat cargo left the port in 1881. One of Portland's largest wheat shippers, Balfour, Guthrie and Co., provided the long awaited opportunity, sending 60,360 bushels of prime Washington wheat to Tacoma for Liverpool delivery by the sailing ship *Dakota*, Captain Isaac Gilkey, master. This first grain cargo was regarded in all quarters as a sure omen of impending good fortune. Bells were rung in Tacoma, ceremonial dinners tendered to the doughty shipmaster; he was even presented a gold watch and chain to memorialize the occasion. Northern Pacific Railway officials freely predicted that Portland's long domination of Pacific Northwest sea-borne commerce would now face successful challenge by Tacoma.

The high hopes of Tacoma's citizens launched by Captain Gilkey's sailing, however, were realized all too slowly. After shipping the solitary wheat cargo in the fall of 1881 only two cargoes of grain left in 1882, Portland shipping 172 the same year. The disappointment in Tacoma was intense. One lone cargo was shipped in 1883 and none at all in 1884. The following year proved slightly more encouraging; three wheat cargoes left Tacoma under hatches in the sailing ships *James P. Drummond*, *Benj. F. Packard*, and the *Artisan*. No grain shipments left the port for twenty-four months during 1886 and 1887. They were disastrous years for Tacoma.

By 1887 the building of the Northern Pacific's main line was nearly completed. Although eagerly anticipated it provided a particular dilemma for Tacomans. The many years in which iron rails for building the railroads had been delivered to their port by sailing ships had been a blessing. They knew all along that when the railroad was completed such shipments would fall off greatly and business at the port would slacken noticeably. With Portland shipping so much Washington grain there were few enough cargoes for ships to carry *away* from Tacoma and now that there was less reason to come at all, long-term prospects were uncertain at best. The few available cargoes of lumber could never be enough to support the port. Only by competing successfully with Portland for grain shipments could Tacoma realize its potential.

The railroad's network of feeder lines could help bring the wheat to Tacoma of course. The great question was could Tacomans store it, mill it, and ship it off their wharves as cheaply and as well as their long-time competitors in Oregon? Only time would reveal the answer. Their record to date was poor and Portlanders trumpeted the wretched figures wherever they could be heard. Whatever advantages lay in Tacoma as a grain port still remained to be proven to unbelieving wheat shippers at Portland.

The lofty-sparred British four-mast bark Queen Margaret, *unusually handsome and universally admired, lies at the Northwestern dock "like a painted ship upon a painted ocean."*

Again the railroad was the key. The Northern Pacific's main line through Stampede Pass was finally completed in June 1887. As Washington's grain farmers increased their use of the new direct route to Tacoma the number of grain shipments began to rise. Twenty-seven ships with grain cargoes cleared the port from 1887 through 1889, carrying over two million bushels of Washington's best wheat. These were at last the kind of statistics Tacomans hungered to see. Impressive as this record was it did not better the three million plus bushels shipped off Portland's wharves the same year. Portland still reigned supreme.

The time had come for further improvements. Major construction was needed. The increasingly large amounts of sacked wheat arriving in Tacoma required expansion of the port's meager facilities. They were then centered in a long, narrow ribbon of water running east and west under the bluff, formerly a channel of the Puyallup River emptying into Commencement Bay. The river had been diverted into a channel a mile to the east and the former channel, dredged and bulkheaded and lined with wharves, was named the City Waterway.

Construction by the Northwestern Improvement Co. (a Northern Pacific Subsidiary) of grain warehouses resulted in a complex of structures along the new waterway, west from the wooden Eleventh Street bridge, loosely bragged about by Tacoma boosters as the "longest warehouse under one continuous roof in the world." This series of buildings along the waterway's south bank was world famous. Cargo handling facilities were eventually added on the wharves, and Tacoma's ability to handle grain

cargoes grew increasingly impressive. Lining the waterway the warehouses became, in time, a solid wall of structures honeycombed with railroad spur tracks and switch points.

By 1900 many Tacomans believed that their port was the largest on Puget Sound for shipping wheat by sea. Their waterfront warehouses could safely store two and a half million bushels of wheat. Tacomans proudly boasted that their mills could grind more flour in a year than the combined mills of Minneapolis and Kansas City. They could assure grain cargoes now to any ships of their steadily enlarging "Grain Fleet." By Hester's time grain left Tacoma in sailing ships with impressive regularity. So many ships called at the port that Tacoma daily newspapers listed their arrivals and departures under the prosaic heading, "The Grain Fleet." The list proved to be a bible for wheat shippers looking for arriving bottoms.

Tacoma was seeing the results of its labors at last. Funds to expand harbor facilities were more readily available. Prospects for business in general seemed better. The outlook for increased grain shipments was so reassuring in 1900 that two well-known, Portland based wheat shippers, Balfour, Guthrie & Co. and Kerr, Gifford & Co., each established branch offices in Tacoma. It was a gesture of confidence that did not pass unnoticed in either Portland or Tacoma.

Between 1893 and 1905 Wilhelm Hester frequented the Tacoma wharves and warehouses almost daily. They appear again and again in his Tacoma photographs. Many of these warehouses were as familiar to the sailing ship seamen as the decks of

the ships that brought them to Tacoma. The warehouses can be identified easily. The immense Northwestern just west of the bridge followed by the London Dock was flanked by the Balfour, Guthrie Dock no. 1. In turn, proceeding westward, were the Oriental Dock, the Commercial Dock, and Coal Bunker no. 5. These familiar landmarks abound in Hester's views of Tacoma.

In Hester's time there always seemed to be sailing vessels waiting to load grain cargoes at the Tacoma warehouse wharves. They were his subjects and their crews his customers. He knew them as well as a shepherd knows his flock. It made no difference to him whether they were British, French, German, or Scandinavian. He was well acquainted with each of them. Their crews were often his friends.

His portraits of the vessels visiting Tacoma include many photographed lying at anchor in Commencement Bay or tied up alongside the grain wharves in the waterway. Hester sought out interesting perspectives from which to make a view, taking his camera to a number of locations close by. His most frequently used vantage points were the northwestern wharves adjacent to the Eleventh Street Bridge and the bridge itself. His photographs reveal that he used several different locations on the bridge's wooden deck. In certain of his bridge views he could only have placed his tripod, securely fixed and braced, on the bridge's wooden center section, a hazardous location. One must marvel at Hester's determination and agility as it could not have been an easy spot for him to reach with his forty pounds of photographic equipment.

Up on the bluff, dominating the waterfront, were Nelson Bennett's famous Tacoma Hotel and the City Hall, the clock in its tall tower chiming every half hour. The original Old Town of Tacoma's earlier days still sprawled under the bluffs, a rabbit warren of muddy streets. The sidewalks were still wooden, the hotels shabby, the saloons unpainted and lurid, and the brothels no less squalid than previously. Notorious Pacific Avenue, running east and west on the overhanging heights, retained its reputation, its forty-odd saloons surviving in sinful glory. Almost everything about Old Town was obscured by the newly built grain warehouses dominating the waterway. But although Tacoma was grown up in many respects it continued to enjoy its original reputation as a tough, wide-open sailor's town.

Even though immense quantities of grain left its wharves Tacoma was not exclusively a grain port. Large shipments of coal from the local mines at Carbonado and Wilkeson left the bay regularly for waiting California markets. Lumber cut in local mills, one of Tacoma's earliest products, had grown to be a major export in 1900. Large cargoes of sawn lumber and timbers left the sawmill wharves in sailing vessels for transport south on coastwise voyages. Sometimes the lumber was carried to Australia, Fiji, China, or Japan. Lumber yards and sawmills lined the south shore of the peninsula for miles, almost as far out to the west as Point Defiance. By 1903 Hanson and Ackerson's famous Old Town mill, possibly Tacoma's oldest sawmill, had been joined by the Tacoma Mill Co., Pacific Shingle, Puget Sound Lumber Co., Tacoma Cedar, Washington Lumber, Reed and Andrews, and a dozen smaller mills.

Near the south shore of Commencement Bay the immense St. Paul Lumber Co. complex wandered over the twelve-square-mile Puyallup tideflats. This newly made land was destined, even then, for Tacoma's eventual port expansion. Hester photographed numbers of American vessels, mainly lumber carrying schooners and barkentines, loading their cargoes of sawn lumber at one or another of Tacoma's busy sawmills.

At the turn of the century Tacomans had good reason to take pride in the port they had created. Through thirty years of sweat and sacrifice they had built a major harbor on Puget Sound, one that would continue to grow in subsequent decades. By 1902 its commerce amounted to 1,818,763 tons valued at $52,371,516. It could no longer be ignored as a major Pacific Coast seaport.

The federal government at that time included Tacoma as one of its legitimate concerns for harbor development on the Pacific Coast assigning the U.S. Corps of Engineers important dredging tasks for additional harbor improvement. This assistance was particularly welcome, lifting the financial burden of port development from the Northern Pacific Railway. It had long assumed the cost and was anxious to be relieved.

Neglected and forgotten, Hester's many glass plates of the Tacoma waterfront lay in their wooden boxes almost unknown for nearly seventy years. Today they are being scrutinized and appreciated by a new audience—scholars, historians, and enthusiasts interested in the port of Tacoma and the magnificent sailing ships that called there. They are among the best images we possess of that vanished time and those long gone trades.

Page 74: In sharp contrast to the ugly sandbank in the foreground, the four-mast bark Lyderhorn, *a powerful example of British sailing ship architecture and construction, creates a maritime portrait of unusual grace.*

Page 75: Enhanced by Hester's masterful use of his wide-angle lens the British full-rigged ship Tamar *is mirrored in the still waters of Commencement Bay.*

Left: The British full-rigged ship Hutton Hall *lies moored between twin symbols of Tacoma's commercial success, logs for·her hungry sawmills and the milling facility of the Centennial Mill Company.*

Below: The British bark Whitlieburn *uses a gasoline-operated endless-belt grain conveyor at the Tacoma wharves. It replaced the slow shouldering of single bags by individual longshoremen, allowing bagged grain to be delivered to a ship's rail with greater dispatch and ease.*

The Ships

The sailing ships calling at Puget Sound ports for lumber and grain cargoes were both a burden and a blessing for young Willi Hester. Photographing them and their crews was his profession and he enjoyed his work. But there were so many of them, and his work was so highly regarded, that he sometimes could not keep up with the demand for his photographs. Tugboats towing these ships in each day from the Pacific Ocean to the west were as busy as ants, darting up and down Commencement Bay, ranging Seattle's many wharves, and touching in at numerous sawmill ports on the way. Arriving or departing, loading their cargoes or repairing sea damage, these tall ships and their crews were Hester's target, his day-to-day bread and butter work. Their numbers seemed endless.

Distinguishing one type of vessel from another was no easy task. To the uninitiated the rigging of a sailing ship seemed a bewildering mass of rope, wire, blocks, and massive wooden and iron spars. Hester himself was no seafaring man; he was a landlubber. But in spite of this limitation he learned fast.

The ships he saw varied in size, carrying capacity, design, construction, ornamentation, and most of all in rig, the number and kinds of sails the vessel carried. Some ships that came to Puget Sound were specifically designed to carry lumber or wheat, others were adapted to the requirements of these trades.

Tacoma's Commencement Bay provided ample anchoring ground for numerous ships. Few presented so handsome a picture as the British full-rigged ship Edenballymore *caught by Willi Hester at anchor early one overcast morning.*

Many square-rigged ships were built with a "tween-deck," a second cargo deck below the main deck. These "tweendecks," or the network of framing throughout the lower hold required to lay such a wooden deck when it was needed, made lumber loading more difficult than in schooners or barkentines, whose unencumbered, cavernous holds were particularly useful for lumber cargoes.

Most wooden schooners and barkentines with their broad decks, wide hatches, and gaping holds were ideally suited for loading and stowing large masses of sawn lumber and longer timbers. Grain was another matter, however. Although it was transported to dockside in burlap bags and was easily stowed in the holds of most sailing vessels, the danger of leakage in wooden hulls proved a serious disadvantage and restricted their use in this trade.

The major distinction in classifying sailing vessels was between those designated as *fore-and-afters*, vessels that carried no yards on which to bend or set square sails, flying only fore-and-aft sails set parallel to the ship's keel, and *square-rigged ships*, which carried many yards and bent square sails to each of them. The yards were normally braced to take advantage of the wind direction and were set at whatever angle to the ship's keel suited the present wind conditions. In following winds from directly behind the ship, astern of her, the yards were laid "square" to the ship's keel or her center line.

Sailing vessels in both of these two categories were built with any number of masts ranging from two to seven. Only those vessels with three, four, or five masts carrying a full suit of square sails on each mast were designated as *ships*. Those with only two masts, similarly rigged with square sails on each mast, were called *brigs*. A two-masted sailing vessel carrying square sails only on its first, or foremast, and fore and aft sails on its second, or aftermast, was called a *hermaphrodite brig*, or in Hester's time on the Pacific Coast a *brigantine*.

Three-, four-, or five-masted vessels that carried full suits of square sails on each of their masts with the exception of the last in line, where fore-and-aft sails were set, were known as *barks*. The number of masts a bark carried preceded its designation, as three-masted bark, four-masted bark, etc.

A popular combination of sails for vessels in the lumber trade on the Pacific Coast was the *barkentine*. Designed to make effective use of the prevailing winds such vessels carried at least three masts, usually not exceeding five, whose foremast alone was rigged with square sails. All the other masts sported a full suit of sails, fore-and-afters consisting of lowers and gaff topsails, as well as staysails between the first and second, the fore and main, masts.

Schooners were vessels of all sizes carrying two to seven masts that normally set *no square sails* but only fore-and-aft sails. In Hester's time many of the lumber carriers in the coastal and deep-sea trades, large schooners, were able to set a temporary square sail on a yard on the foremast for help in following winds only. This sail served as no more than an adjunct to the regular suit of fore-and-aft sails and did not affect its correct designation as schooner rigged.

Shimmering in the warmth of the afternoon sun the British four-mast bark Manchester *reveals the engineered strength required by sailing ships to safely carry heavy cargoes of grain and lumber to the world's seaports.*

The design and construction of the hulls of these sailing vessels did not affect their designation of type. Any of these variations in sailing ship rig could be found on hulls built of wood, iron, or steel. In all cases the designation derived *only* from the number of masts and the type of sails set, the masting and rigging.

Hester soon learned to tell one rig from another. In time he could recognize many individual vessels by name. He also found that those who worked on the waterfront had their own way of describing things. It was common, for instance, for the carrying capacity of sailing vessels, their tonnage, formally reckoned in figures, to be discussed in terms of the number of days needed for the stevedore crews to load and stow a full cargo. Understanding such expressions was essential for the young photographer as he moved among the wharves.

Hester photographed the sailing ships wherever he found them. Made fast to a Tacoma wharf in the City Waterway or anchored to a buoy in the stream in the lee of Brown's Point, it made little difference. He taught himself how to photograph them to their best advantage, valuing the photogenic qualities he found in the quiet of a chilly morning or the stillness of a flat calm at Commencement Bay.

Often he was obliged to follow the ships wherever they needed to go to carry on their work. One day he might go south to Puget Sound's great drydock on Vashon Island, at Dockton, to catch the power of their massive hulls looming high over his head. Sometimes he would stumble on an image so powerful he could not pass it by, even though he might not sell it. The drama of the huge steel bark seen on page 22 careened one grey day on Blakely Bay's north shore beach was such an instance.

The photograph most often called for by his customers was the broadside view, every spar and every line on the ship setting properly and secured by a proud mate and a hard-working crew. Hester quickly mastered the art of photographing ships from this perspective. As time went by, he grew increasingly sensitive to the many possibilities for photographing them in new and exciting fashions. Fully loaded or empty, in ballast, awaiting cargoes of lumber and grain, each ship represented a new challenge to the eager young photographer. Each commission seemed to trigger his artistic responses. He was learning to see and feel the beauty of these sailing vessels as their crews saw and felt it.

Any comparison between his ship portraits and those of his competitors offers evidence of the difference in his treatment. Unfailingly he managed to discover a point of beauty in each ship he photographed. Witness the blunt power of the great, iron, four-masted bark on page 87, the handsome energy of the British full-rigged ship on page 82. Whether recording the handy grace of a dainty little bark or the powerful beauty of a wooden schooner, its decks groaning with a load of lumber fourteen feet high, he made his unwieldy 8″ × 10″ glass plates with professional ease.

Willi Hester did not avoid the rough weather so frequently encountered at Puget Sound. He accepted it and made sensitive use of the shifting light, overcast skies, fallen snow, and leaden rain as natural counterpoints to the local scene he was photographing. In this he was more daring, more innovative, than many of his fellow photographers. Taking full advantage of the available light, even under difficult conditions, he created images of striking clarity while at the same time capturing the subtle nuances of tone, texture, mood, and place.

Whatever its emotional or psychological roots, Hester's sensibility was that of an artist. More intuitive than deliberate, his art is perhaps nowhere better expressed than in his portraits of sailing ships. The few plates reproduced here reveal this young photographer at his poetic best.

Left: Although the British four-mast bark Walter Wilson *did not visit Commencement Bay often, when she did her lean and lofty power occasioned admiration and laudatory newspaper articles. Her mate, remembering the* Andelana's *capsizing here, has sent down her three skysail yards rather than risk increasing her tenderness in Tacoma's dangerously windy bay.*

Right: Hester found this classically beautiful quartering view of the British four-mast bark Samaritan *at anchor in Commencement Bay following a heavy snow. He had learned that most sailing ships benefited greatly when photographed at this angle.*

Page 84: Rowed around his vessel by the ship's apprentices the Forteviot's *mate assures himself that each yard is braced square, every line properly taut and secured, the whole a model of nautical precision. Only then would he permit Hester to photograph his charge.*

Page 85: Under tow of the sidewheeler Multnomah, *doubling as a tugboat, the four-topmast schooner* Endeavour *is bound for the Port Blakely mills to top off her lumber cargo partially loaded at Tacoma's nearby sawmills.*

Left: Sea damage repaired, the Swedish four-mast bark Svithiod, *purchased by her owners to help train young Swedish officers, awaits the arrival of tugs to tow her up Sound to Tacoma's wharves.*

Right: The size and heavy construction of the British four-mast bark Prince Robert *are dramatized by contrast with dockyard workmen, assembled at Hester's request, below her looming steel hull.*

Page 88: Her glory days behind her, the wooden bark Admiral Tregethoff *now carries only lumber for a living. Beset by interminable leaking she must rely on a windmill pump to save the energies of her small crew. Without it they would be unable to carry on ship's work, too quickly exhausted by the endless labor of pumping ship.*

Page 89: Hauled out for repairs, the British four-mast bark Marion Frazer *sits high on her blocks in the steam-powered drydock at Dockton, in Quartermaster Harbor on Vashon Island. Built for Port Townsend investors and sold to new owners after that town's real estate debacle, the massive dock, the largest on Puget Sound at that time, rendered important service for many years to Puget Sound shipping.*

Left: Bound for the Hawaiian Islands the four-mast barkentine Makaweli *lies in ballast in Tacoma's Commencement Bay waiting the call to load her lumber cargo at the nearby sawmills.*

Right: The four-mast barkentine Thos. P. Emigh *idles at a Tacoma wharf with a twelve-foot-high deckload of sawn lumber securely chained and turnbuckled for delivery to ports in Southern California. Her route lies northwest through Puget Sound to Cape Flattery, then due south into the stormy North Pacific.*

Deck Views

Most of Hester's deck views were photographed from aft on the poop deck, near the ship's steering wheel, looking forward. This area, the poop, was the home of the ship's afterguard, her officers. It was accepted without question as the point of command marking the physical separation of territories claimed separately by the ship's officers and her sailors. No one walked this special domain, the poop, except to labor when bidden or by the rarely tendered invitation of the officers. One and all, sailor and landlubber alike, regarded this part of the sailing ship as near-sacred.

One expects to find a shipmaster on his own poop—where else? Hester has included him in these views where he belongs. Sometimes we see him alone or joined by his wife, children, or the family pet, sometimes by all of them. On occasion he stands with his junior officers, carefully selected business associates, or a party of shoreside friends. Often the master might entertain whatever colleagues were with him in port at the time.

No single stereotype applies to all these men. Although as shipmasters they shared common pressures and responsibilities, each was an individual and responded in his own way to Hester's camera. Among his British and German subjects were many

The damp decks of the German ship Ariadne *reveal the complexity of a sailing ship's rigging and equipment. Secured and shipshape, her gear is a fitting complement to her bearded captain leaning stiffly on the companionway leading to her cabin below.*

who faced the lens resolutely, firm and unyielding in their acceptance of the responsibilities of command at sea. They struck no playful poses for either the photographer or the folks at home. They appear in certain cases to be truculent and impatient with the picture-taking process, as though in some way it represented an affront to their dignity. Their jobs were not easy. Command required them to maintain in their relationships a clearly defined line, a strict boundary, which no man might cross at any time. Though they could be winning in manner or jolly as circumstances required, they were, first of all, stern men unwilling to play games. They allowed no liberties they had not granted.

While they were no less fine seamen for all their casual manners, many of the French and Italian shipmasters portrayed by Hester in these deck views seem to be more at ease than their British and German counterparts, lounging in comfort instead of standing stiffly. They create the impression of having paused but momentarily in their day's work to face the photographer.

Photographed with wide-angle lenses these unique deck views are remarkable for the wealth of information they offer about sailing ship construction. Revealed in the crispest detail are ancient rigging practices and seafaring lore all but forgotten today. The accumulated know-how of generations of shellbacks, "sailorizing" as practiced by masters, is on display in these images.

One cannot help but sense in these views the pride taken in these ships by the men who served them so faithfully. The evidence of their patient work reinforces the oft-told tales of the curious love

relationship between seamen of the sail and their ships. Look at their well-scrubbed decks. Note how carefully they are maintained. Everything in these deck views speaks of attention and constant care. Gleaming paintwork, well-varnished wooden structures, polished brass, carefully tended lines: each item gives witness to the respect and devotion these ships commanded.

Page 94: In typical raw and wet Blakely weather it is no wonder this portly shipmaster, white collared and togged out in his shoregoing derby, up on his poop for his portrait by Hester, ducks behind the chart house of his command, the German four-mast bark Lisbeth.

Page 95: The master of the British ship Cortez, *his lady, the mates, and the cabin steward pose for a group portrait, mindful of anxious friends back home who will receive copies of this photograph. Hester's image of the group posed in studied ease around the teak companionway and the minute gun (the tiny saluting cannon on deck to the left) will provide awaited reassurance.*

Left: A cigar in one hand and binoculars in the other complete the businesslike adornments of this young ship-master standing alongside the deep-sea log reel at the break of the poop. His unpressed shore rig, rumpled from long storage at the bottom of his sea bag, verify him as a seafarer not a visiting landlubber.

Right: A flower in one's buttonhole although dapper was not the approved dress for most seamen in Hester's day. In this photograph, however, these stern-faced officers of the flush-decked, full-rigged British ship *Bermuda* sport boutonnières in their lapels as they stand ready to receive visitors with classic British aplomb.

Page 98: On a cold winter day in Tacoma, a seagoing family dressed in their heavy clothing huddle beside the chart house on the British four-mast bark *Mozambique.*

Page 99: Captain McKinnon, "Angus if you please, Sir," master of the British full-rigged ship *Belford,* steadies himself for Willi Hester's camera, requiring no more than the chart house to support his stiffened back, his stern-faced mate close at hand, and his beloved dog at his feet.

Left: The broad decks of the German four-mast bark Wandsbek, *massive and powerful, were built to withstand shattering seas and gale force winds, guaranteeing that her deadweight cargoes would be delivered safely, a promise reinforced by the strong construction of her spars and rigging.*

Right: Caught up in the easy mood of two French seafarers aboard their vessel, Hester manages to capture their relaxed attitude perfectly, his image a triumph of casual ease.

Page 102: Built to carry lumber on her broad decks the newly launched five-mast schooner George E. Billings *completes her fitting out at her building site, the Hall Brothers Blakely yard. Her master, a rough and ready type, is impatient to get away to sea, not pose foolishly for a fussy photographer.*

Page 103: Three German shipmasters meet on the standard compass bridge of a sister ship, the four-mast bark Alsterberg, *newly arrived from Hamburg. They can depend on her master for news of the old country, a hospitable glass of schnapps, and a bit of the sentimentality so dear to German hearts.*

Captains and Crews

These photographs of sailing ship crews are not portraits of tramps or of just any group of workmen dressed in shabby, ill-fitting clothes. They are portraits of working seamen, highly skilled tradesmen, experts in their chosen craft, dressed as they had to be for their work. They introduce us to sea-wanderers, men who were willing to forego the security of life ashore and the pleasure of their families and friends to help deliver the world's goods in sailing ships. Theirs was a hard and dangerous life. Sailing ship men expected to be gone from their homes for months and their voyages sometimes lasted for several years. The perils of the sea were such that many of them never returned from their voyages, lost somewhere at sea. These little-known nomads were the seamen of the sail.

The men and boys who formed these crews were not uniform; no two of them were stamped from a common mold. They were a body of individuals of many nationalities, as diverse as any other group of men brought together to do the world's work. They were united by their individual backgrounds, varied pasts, and singular temperaments. Among

For each man in this photograph, death waited twenty-three icy fathoms below at the muddy bottom of Commencement Bay. Only a few hours after Hester made the negative, this ship, the British four-mast bark Andelana, *newly arrived from China, capsized in gale winds during the night, drowning most of her crew and officers.*

them were the unlettered, even the ignorant, and the highly educated. Their stations in life and their outlooks, their prejudices and their passions, ranged from the dispossessed to the most fortunate. Age was no barrier. The standards for crew selection made room for those newcomers wishing to learn the sailor's craft and thus wise old heads, able seamen, and greenhorns worked side by side.

It is necessary to peer behind their unkempt beards and shabby clothing to see serious, sober, hard-working men proud of their abilities to work their great ships through deep waters. These are the faces of working men, taken where they work. They present an unvarnished glimpse of the real life seafarer serving real ships. Such men have been seen too infrequently. To most of their contemporaries they were strangers, as they still are to us today.

Observe the group of men portrayed on page 104. Look at them very closely. They are part of the crew of the bark *Andelana.* Together with their master, Captain George Staling, they sit, alive and warm, grouped on their broad main deck. Even the ship's pets, their dogs, pose with them. It was the afternoon of 14 January 1899, the last day they would live. Of course, they didn't know it; no one did.

Their huge bark had arrived at Tacoma after a wintry passage from China, anchored, discharged her ballast, and was waiting to load her promised cargo, 3,500 tons of grain for the United Kingdom. She was ready. Her holds were empty, swept clean. Easy to capsize without ballast to stiffen her the *Andelana* was helped to remain upright at her anchorage by large floating ballast logs chained to her hull on both sides. The long dark night that followed witnessed several vicious gales from the southwest.

In the morning although the ballast logs still floated the *Andelana* had vanished. She was gone, capsized and fast in the mud at the bottom of Commencement Bay, twenty-three fathoms below. Sixteen of her crew perished, drowned in their bunks, with almost no warning for the sleeping sailors. Not a single man in this photograph survived.

Perhaps no other photograph remains to remember any of them. For their families or friends this photograph of Hester's may be the only surviving link with a parent, a brother, or a treasured shipmate lost to the sea.

Although these crew photographs seem dominated by rough-looking men of all nationalities they tell another story as well. They reveal another side of these sailors' difficult lives, a softer side. One can pick out some of the unsophisticated pleasures these men enjoyed aboard the vessels, joys far different than the lurid moments they bought in the waterfront saloons and brothels as long as their money lasted.

Animals and birds have always been welcome pets aboard sailing ships. They fulfilled a variety of human needs. Cats were popular for their rat-hunting abilities, dogs for their loyal friendliness. Singing birds reaffirmed the land for sailors, a sweet reminder of their other lives. Pets were cared for with great tenderness and highly esteemed. Several of these pets can be seen lovingly cradled in their owners' arms in the photographs reproduced on pages 110 and 115.

The watches below for off-duty seamen encouraged some sailors to build ship models. Fair weather was a necessity for the delicate work required, although great precision was difficult on a moving ship at sea. Most such models while ingeniously constructed were crudely fashioned. Nevertheless they were prized by some as accurate examples of the modeled ships' rigging. Most sailors knew the details of their own ship's rigging more intimately than the shape of their vessel's underwater body. Sailors' models appear in these crew photographs in all sizes and shapes, from a tiny waterline model capable of being held in one hand to a large replica of the four-mast bark *Lynton* encased in glass.

There were artisans among these crews, men with special skills incorporating the cunning of generations of their fellows. Their endeavors included such crafts as sailmaking and carpentry of the kind needed aboard a sailing ship. Known as daymen, for they slept the night through at sea and stood no watches, these men were honored by their shipmates for their special competence. Their simple pride is understandable. In the photographs reproduced on pages 112 and 108 the sailmaker and the carpenter proudly display the symbols of their crafts. In one case it is a bolt of new sail canvas and in the other it is the carpenter's saw held stiffly across its owner's chest. In the crew portrait on page 113 including the master's wife, a potted plant at her feet marks her particular contribution to the ship's well-being.

When time in port allowed, both officers and seamen relaxed with whatever pleasures their rough environments made possible. Those who could made music; those who couldn't sang along. Music had always lightened the work at sea and lifted the heart as well. It was also greatly appreciated in port. Accordions and banjos were both popular. Fewer seamen could play fiddles and horns, but these instruments too were favored among crews as the photograph on page 121 demonstrates.

Shipmasters, unlike seamen, had the means and the credit ashore to organize small celebrations on board their vessels. On page 120 Hester has caught the high point in one such soiree aboard a French bark. It is complete, after the fashion of the day, with fancy dress, raised glasses, smiles, and female companionship any sailor would envy.

Seamen were by and large industrious and time wasted was frowned upon. Many shipmasters and some sailors sewed, knitted, and carpentered with considerable skill. Others raised plants, cared for pets, kept diaries, painted pictures, or made photographs at sea. On page 115 we see pipe-smoking Captain Alex Teschner, master of the German bark *Pera*, proudly wearing the result of what might have been his own handiwork or that of his sailmaker, a homemade, full length oilskin coat, worn for protection in heavy weather.

Certain shipmasters enjoyed the formalities of their rank and dressed the part on every occasion. Others were happy only in work clothes, tar stained and paint streaked. Those who dressed up were given to brass-bound blue coats and trousers, visored caps emblazoned with their company badges, stiff collars and black ties. Captain Edward Gates-James,

R.N.R., a tough seaman of the old school, was one such. A hard taskmaster he set his crew a stern example. Demanding but concerned he is said to have customarily had his steward serve tea and cakes to the mates at the change of watches. Seated with his officers and apprentices on page 118 he symbolizes the fatherly rectitude frequently found among sailing ship masters.

A sterling example of a shipmaster of a different sort is shown in the photograph reproduced on page 122 of Captain Georg Cringler, master of the German ship *Flottbek*, with his assembled family and dog. A splendid seamen, a hard driver of his ship, he created a kind and agreeable atmosphere aboard the *Flottbek* reflected in the photograph of her skylarking crew reproduced on page 121.

Typical of sailing ship seamen is the crew assembled at the break of the poop, reproduced on page 114. These are the true sea dogs, confident men, strong men, arms folded, ready for whatever comes their way. Even the ship's boy at the far right puts on his sternest expression to face the photographer.

Shipmasters of a different stripe are reproduced on page 116. These two "jolly tars" seem to enjoy being photographed as shore-going dandies. Perhaps we see them merely dressed for relaxation with a friend, a bottle of beer, and a card game aboard their own vessels. They could be bachelors or married men, their families left ashore, at home.

It was a matter of pride for those shipmasters who carried their families to sea with them, or even for those whose families visited with them in port, to pose their smaller children for their photograph alongside the ship's wheel. Few things aboard a sailing vessel better symbolized to a seaman the control of his destiny than a working ship's wheel. What more appropriate omen of future good fortune for a sailor's child?

It is appealing to note the youthful innocence with which young apprentices in the photographs reproduced on pages 106 and 112 mimic their officers, dressing up in stiff white collars and freshly pressed clothing, cap visors polished, company badges on their caps ablaze with color after cleaning. Together with the ship's boys whose job was to help the stewards and the cooks, these fresh-faced apprentices, officers in training, seem incapable of enduring the rough environment of a commercial sailing ship.

One often found singular types among sailors, men who were especially powerfully built or whose strong countenances projected great self-confidence. The appearance of some men was so dramatic that they demanded more than a single casual glance. If it were life's intention to imitate art the tall, black seaman wearing a derby hat on page 111 would be a splendid example. Here standing with his shipmates, he looks as though he were indeed the prototype of Joseph Conrad's tragic hero James Wait, seaman of the ship *Narcissus.*

A unique quality in these crew photographs is their informality, the almost casual manner in which the seamen, posing for their portraits, dispose themselves. Most similar views by other photographers are more studied, more rigidly posed groupings. The sailors seem less alive, more robot-like. They lack the spontaneity and liveliness, the animated postures and expressions, that can be seen in Hester's photographs. Hester had an uncommon gift for putting seamen at their ease. His intense empathy with them and with the seafarer's life dominates his images. In the warmth of these photographs lies much of their appeal.

Page 110: Next to a dependable shipmate nothing could command more loyalty and affection from the average windjammer sailor than an animal or a bird. The British four-mast bark Lynton *had more than her share. In 1891 her floating menagerie included two dogs, a cat, and a bird, probably a young parrot.*

Page 111: These British seamen, black and white, form the afterguard of the four-mast bark Kate Thomas. *Since British sailing ships were required by law to serve watered lime juice regularly to their crews to ward off scurvy, it was inevitable they would be called "limejuicers," their crews "limeys."*

Page 112: Sailors were serious men who took great pride in their craftsmanship. No one dared question the choice of the Boadecia's *sailmaker to bring a roll of his best Dundee sailcloth to the picture-taking session as a symbol of his craft.*

Page 113: The air of domesticity in port surrounding white-bearded Captain Jones, master of the bark Lady Isabella, *belies the sternness of this autocratic Welsh sea dog. A potted plant at Mrs. Jones's feet, the single stemmed plant to her right, and the elan of the cook and cabin steward in their white hats each add to the impression of bonhomie.*

Br. Ship Boadicea, Capt. Robt. Roberts.

WM. HESTER, Marine Photo.

SHIP LADY ISABELLA.
J. WYNNE JONES, Commander.

614 Front Street,
SEATTLE, WASH.

Left: Portraits of German sailing ship crews are usually, with a few notable exceptions, models of straightforward efficiency, no frills, no skylarking, little merriment of any kind. This view, every sailor alert, in cloth hats and leather boots, arms folded, reveals Hester at his best among his kameraden.

Dressed properly for business ashore and with his pet dogs on his lap, Captain Gates-James appears in this formal portrait to be a typical Victorian English gentleman, a different sort of human being than the tough sea dog remembered by those who knew him professionally.

Foul weather on Puget Sound offered Captain Alex Teschner of the German bark Pera a chance to put on the new coat his sailmaker had just completed for him. The captain's stiff white collar, knotted four-in-hand tie, and rough oiled coat were strange companions for a sailor in any weather.

This bluff sea captain took a bride and together they produced this handsome child, their son. After sailing round Cape Horn aboard the British four-mast bark Kinrosshire, they reached Puget Sound, where Willi Hester took this picture.

Sailing ship masters might be tyrants, figures of fatherly solicitude, or they could carry on as little gods on their own quarterdecks if they so desired. In port some emerged with new personalities, strange manners, and unlikely dress. No two shipmasters offer more convincing proof than these comrades-in-arms "dandied up" for a party ashore in Tacoma.

One smiles shyly at the camera while the other beckons with her smouldering eyes, offering a lucky escort the promise of excitement ashore. Bewinged and befeathered these two Tacoma visitors spice up an otherwise dull day for sailors and photographer alike.

Page 118: Few of Hester's photographs demonstrate so well the balance of reserve and affection marking the professional relationships between an old-school British shipmaster and his junior officers and apprentices as this group portrait of Captain Edward Gates-James, R.N.R., and the afterguard of the four-mast bark Lynton.

Page 119: As shipmasters were generally conservative it was a rare bird that would dress up in a straw hat, a plaid cap, or a spotted tie. Wilhelm Hester rounded up an unusual group in this charming picture of visiting officers.

This joyous image may record a birthday, a national holiday, a newly born child, or nothing more than a long-delayed reunion of old friends. Good beer, maybe a fine wine, fancy clothes, fair weather, and the willing photographer transform a normal day aboard the French bark Lamorciere into a memorable one.

While primitive bands were common among sailing ship crews, so professional a group as the one assembled here on the main deck of the German ship Flottbek was not. These sailor-musicians prepare an impromptu concert for the photographer, the jolly steward keeping time with his square-faced bottle of Holland gin.

The crew of the German ship Flottbek *knew Captain Georg Cringler as a "driver," a sailor who pushed his ship at sea along in any kind of wind or weather, day or night. Few realized how much he cherished family life, taking his brood to sea and visiting friends from the old country wherever he could find them.*

Remarkably poised and sober-faced this sea captain's daughter adopts a familiar stance for the photographer, the "man at the wheel" pose, one she has seen every day of her life aboard her father's command.

Shipmasters' Cabins

The busy maritime world in which sailing ships carried out their work has been photographed abundantly. Very few facets have been ignored. The ships, their officers and crews, their decks at sea and in port—everything about them has been photographed. Only one view has been missing, the interior of the captain's quarters. This very private home at sea, called a saloon, cabin, or the Old Man's quarters, was very seldom photographed. The interior views made by Hester are the only such images in existence.

While the lack of such views remains a puzzle a few explanations may shed some light on their rarity. The captain's cabin was first of all a very private domain, a closely guarded small world encompassing the captain's life and his family's as well, if they accompanied him aboard his vessel. Tradition required him to rule this kingdom with unbending firmness. It was an autocracy, sometimes benevolent, sometimes otherwise. It was a region completely off limits to most persons and accessible by special dispensation to only a few. As the captain maintained a life rigorously private from his officers and crew, his private quarters below the poop deck were even more so.

Captain and Mrs. Edward Gates-James maintained their cabin aboard the British four-mast bark Lynton *no differently than their Victorian home ashore. Everything was in proper order, spotlessly clean, rubbed down, polished and gleaming in fresh varnish and new paint. Each day in port, promptly at four in the afternoon as in their parlor at home, tea and cakes were served in the cabin.*

There were no electric lights on a sailing ship and any area below decks was dark and difficult to photograph without additional light. In the case of the master's cabin only the cabin skylight, overhead on the poop deck, afforded whatever natural light was available, requiring long time exposures and stiffer than normal poses. In making these saloon views Hester may have used primitive flash powder, a device that alarmed many of those persons required to face it. The possibility of fire below decks from its use was especially dreaded by many shipmasters. The reasons were obvious.

Because these intimate photographs were mainly of interest to the captains involved, the sales possibilities were more limited than the usual Hester photographs of the ships and their crews. It is possible that Hester made them mainly as a bribe to secure the captains' permission to make the additional photographs that were his bread and butter.

The Victorian elegance of some of these shipmasters' cabins can be misleading in that they were furnished so lavishly only when the vessel was expected in port for a long stay. Very few of the freestanding items seen in these photographs could withstand the pitching and tossing of a sailing vessel in heavy weather. The destruction of most loose items, *anything* not firmly secured, was assured in the great seas of the Howling Fifties or off the pitch of the Horn in strong winds.

The characteristic look of a cabin at sea is best revealed in the sparsely furnished cabin shown on page 132, where we find the captain playing cards with a select few of his fellow shipmasters. The barren utility revealed in this photograph is more typical of the cabin of a bachelor shipmaster or a married man at sea without his family than one maintained by a captain's wife at sea. Each cabin Hester photographed offers different examples of the bric-a-brac and memorabilia reminding the shipmaster of his life ashore or perhaps the life he dreamed might be his in retirement. In the view reproduced on page 126 stands a small piano organ, along with several strongly-built, overstuffed captain's chairs. In another shown on page 137 the cabin of this British ship reveals a cane rocker, a business-like rolltop desk for the conduct of ship's business, a lute, a heavily embossed book, a red chintz lampshade for the overhead kerosene lamp, ornate pillows (in one chair the American flag decorates a pillow), the omnipresent birdcage in the well of the skylight, and Hester's mounted photographs of the ship herself flanking the sideboard mirror.

In the photograph of the *Balmoral's* cabin, reproduced on page 138, souvenirs of many journeys crowd the fireplace mantel, oriental fans, South Sea shells, vases, beads, metal platters, etc. The heavy water carafe, ready glasses, and silver tea service suggest the hospitality extended to selected guests of the shipmaster and his wife. They might entertain with musical duets, implied by the piano at the rear of the cabin and the mandolins on the table. The Turkish rugs covering the deck obscure the plain pine planks more easily seen once the ship is at sea.

The *Forteviot's* grand cabin, reproduced on page 139, suggests the master carried his children aboard. A hobby horse and an Angoura goat, each mounted on wheels, could not be more appreciated by sea-weary children on a long deep-sea passage. They stand mute guard over a magnificent tiled fireplace overloaded with photos of family and friends. A ship model, built perhaps by a crew member as a gift for the captain's son, stands atop a book on the cabin table. At the rear of the cabin a violin, sheet music on its portable stand, and a shawl-draped piano await some festive occasion. Reigning over the scene in patriotic splendor, above the fireplace, are the crossed flags of Great Britain and the United States. The heavy figured drapes, the lavish oriental rugs, the heavy tablecloth, and the fringed glass shade shielding the classic, hanging kerosene lamp form a characteristic picture of many shipmasters' saloons while in port.

The sitting room of the *Eva Montgomery,* a British ship shown on page 136, provides a detailed view of the combination of professional and personal items typical of so very many captains' living quarters. Each piece of nautical gear needed by the captain is carefully stowed in its proper place, ready for use. The overhead telltale compass hangs in its gimbals in the well of the skylight. This convenient arrangement allowed the shipmaster at work, below in his cabin, to check the compass course kept by the man at the wheel on deck above his head. The ornate but precise barometer and chronometer hang in solemn splendor on the bulkhead. Below them two long glasses rest in homemade wooden racks, small evidence of a skillful carpenter aboard.

In sharp contrast the master's wife hangs her canary and its art deco cage from the overhead, and a newly purchased bicycle stands in the corner of the cabin to be carried round Cape Horn for the children waiting at home. Fresh flowers fill glass vases on a lace covered table. Framed pictures abound as do soft pillows. A portable heater to fight off the sea's chill and a jar of the captain's favorite tobacco, Plug Cut, complete the Victorian splendor so typical of such cabins.

Two particular photographs must not be missed; they are one-of-a-kind rarities. The first, reproduced on page 134, shows us a picture of the captain's stateroom, his sleeping quarters, aboard the British four-mast bark *Lynton.* This is the heart of his domain. Here, surrounded by many mementos of his "other" life, the captain snatches the hurried rests he allows himself at sea. They are a necessary and welcome respite from the long, demanding hours he spends on deck providing the leadership required to keep his vessel moving along safely.

It is touching to witness in this photograph the small indulgences revealing the man inside the shipmaster. Photographs of brothers, sisters, and numerous relatives crowd his sideboard. Above the head of his bed framed pictures of his father and mother stand symbolic guard. Locked behind curtained glass doors are the books that form his library, faithful companions on long voyages. Velvet covered weights on his table are used to hold their pages in place against the uncertain motion of a sailing ship under way. The heavy drapes that curtain his bunk are reminders of how preciously sound sleep at sea was cherished. Even the stuffed owl, near the overhead,

scowls, a silent sentinel over this private seagoing home. We are looking in this photograph at a sight few persons have ever seen, then or now.

Far different in all respects, but no less guarded, was the half deck, the traditional home of the ship's youthful apprentices, reproduced on page 135. This small metal house on the main deck, often no more than ten feet by ten feet, provided a rough home affording wooden bunks as sleeping accommodations for six to eight apprentices. Wooden lockers as shown on the rear bulkhead and a simple wooden table, a rough plank affair bisecting the cramped quarters, completed the minimum furniture provided. Shipowners spent no money for anything they considered needless luxury. The few evidences in this rare photograph of order and elegance were "in port" niceties. One would find few table coverings at sea, and the framed painting of the ship, the *Lynton,* on the forward bulkhead would have been safely stowed away to protect its glass. Flowers in a dish were never found in the half deck and hanging curtains with silk tiebacks were pure extravagance. The rough pine benches flanking the port and starboard bunks are far more typical of the real-life half deck at sea than this curtained and stenciled "in port" photograph of Hester's.

The sextant on the covered table and the binoculars are two mute symbols of the apprentices' hope that their four-year stint of work and study would win them second mate certificates. Below the white-painted lockers at the left is a supply of fresh-baked ship's bread, the soft variety as opposed to the hated hardtack. For most sailors, apprentices as well as seamen, it was an unaccustomed luxury at sea. Few photographs taken by Hester so clearly reveal the softening touches sailors brought with them to sea. Such luxuries were needed to blunt the hardship, pain, loneliness, and boredom of their long voyages.

Look hard at the photograph on page 133 of the sailmaker of the British four-mast bark *Pegasus*. He is a shellback of the old school and the craft he plies is an ancient one. In this unique photograph details of sailmaking known to but very few are revealed in abundance. Rolls of new canvas, Arbroath flax, their best storm canvas, lie on the deck against the steel bulkhead of the sailmaker's cabin. Strands of marlin hang from a wooden shelf over the sailmaker's head. The shelf is loaded with the tools he needs: beeswax to ease his twine through tough canvas, a spirit lamp to soften the wax in freezing weather, and a handmade ditty bag for whatever scraps of rope yarn and canvas he can save. "Waste not want not" is his slogan. Even his handmade canvas cap is testimony to his parsimony and his self reliance.

The man is himself a study. His worn and gnarled hands, one encased in his sailmaker's palm, are busy sewing rope grommets in the sail on his lap and at his feet. This cabin is his home. Apart from the maze of rigging aloft that bears his handiwork, this is his private world. Behind him, his blanket laden hammock, sagging from the overhead, marks him as a true oldtimer. Beside it, on deck, stands his handmade sea chest topped by a few books. Many sailmakers took their books with them to sea. Rarely indeed did one find an illiterate sailmaker. Somehow each of them found considerable time to read, and they always seemed to search out at least one young sailor to encourage to do likewise.

If Hester had taken no other photographs than these few warmly intimate cabin views his work would deserve to endure. They are the very heart of his legacy.

Left: Time in port hung heavy and a card playing, cigar smoking, whiskey drinking evening organized by the master of the Abyssinia for his bachelor colleagues relieved the boredom pleasantly. The mandolin, caged canary, and fresh flowers were unusual accouterments in such surroundings.

Few craftsmen aboard a sailing ship were more greatly needed or appreciated than a competent sailmaker. In spartan simplicity this sailmaker in his meager quarters aboard the British four-mast bark Pegasus cuts and repairs the great canvas sails entrusted to his skilled care.

Page 134: Cluttered with prized mementos of his life ashore the captain's cabin of the Lynton exhibits the happy evidence of one Victorian sea dog's private life.

Page 135: Off the pitch of the Horn in wild weather the overhead of this half deck, the apprentices' home, would leak furiously, its sodden steel bulkheads running wet. As the ship rolled heavily the floating sea chests would "come adrift," adding danger. The curtains, flowers, and table coverings seen here were luxuries reserved for port. Who wouldn't sell a farm and go to sea?

While in port, shipmasters' wives vied with each other to create Victorian extravaganzas aboard their floating homes. Sea-stained carpets, lace curtains, heavy drapes, silken pillows, couch covers, and gilded mirrors were taken out of storage and placed in familiar corners. Although carefully planned, the whole amounted to a confusion of popular geegaws and highly prized bric-a-brac.

Right: A bird cage swings from the overhead as does a silk-curtained kerosene lamp. A polished rolltop desk (for ship's business) flanks a small piano itself confronted by a wicker rocker piled high with souvenir pillows. Magazines, leather-bound photograph albums, and musical instruments decorate the tops of carpeted tables. It is a maze of compact comfort. There is much to see . . . look for yourself!

Page 138: The Balmoral's *cabin is dressed for expected guests. Drinks, decanters, and a silver tea service await their servers. Sheet music trembles on the pianoforte rack; mandolins and banjos, tuned and ready, stand in the cabin corners. The stove, a masterpiece of glazed tile, awaits only a lit match (Britons call them lucifers) to ward off Tacoma's wet chill.*

Page 139: Piano and violin occupy prominent positions in the Forteviot's *cabin. The captain and his wife were both accomplished musicians. Only a very few shipmasters played musical instruments, usually practicing in private and maintaining their musical enthusiasm a deeply held family secret.*

Notes on the Photographs

Reliable information on sailing ships arriving at or departing from Puget Sound ports in the years 1893 through 1906 is incomplete. In consequence some dates noted here may be in error. For the same reason the identification of some vessels, particularly deck views and photos of cabins, can only be tentative at this point. Because of the time lag between changes in command and the documentation of those changes in a printed record, the names of particular masters may be erroneous here as well.

Assistance is needed to accurately identify and date these photographs. Any help will be gratefully appreciated.

Numbers given below refer to pages on which illustrations appear.

PRELIMINARIES

2   Seattle, Elliott Bay, 1895. Three-mast ship *Dalgonar*, Captain J. Kitchen
6   Tacoma, 1904. Four-mast bark *Austrasia*, Captain W. Ewart

INTRODUCTION

10   Port Blakely, 1905. From left to right: four-mast bark *Englehorn*, Captain E. H. Lovitt; four-mast bark *Bracadale*, Captain H. J. S. Youlden; three-mast bark *Albania*, ex *City of Glasgow*, Captain J. Christensen; four-mast bark *Wanderer*, Captain T. Dunning; four-mast schooner *Lyman D. Foster*, Captain D. O. Killman; five-mast schooner *Crescent*, Captain T. Olson
12   Tacoma, Commencement Bay, 1895. Four-mast schooner *Meteor*, Captain E. Björn

Adding a novel touch to this crew photograph, Hester has posed the Lynton *"boys" at the break of the poop around a newly completed model of their four-mast bark. The model will probably be traded, ashore in Tacoma, to a willing barkeep for a few rounds of liquor.*

16   Port Blakely from the south shore, 1904. Four-mast bark *Beechbank*, Captain J. R. Brenmer at far right
18   Port Blakely. Vessel and date unidentified
20   Tacoma, Commencement Bay, 1899. Four-mast bark *Drumblair*, Captain H. Davies
22   Port Blakely north shore, 1893. Four-mast bark *Andrina*, Captain W. Smith
23   Tacoma, 1904. Four-mast bark *Balmoral*, Captain J. E. Roop
24   Tacoma, 1903. Three-mast ship *Eva Montgomery*, Captain G. Harrison
28   Port Blakely. Vessel and date unidentified
29   Tacoma, 1903. Four-mast bark *Ecuador*, ex *Snaigow*, Captain O. Dickmann
30   Seattle, 1902. Vessel unknown
34   Tacoma. Commencement Bay, 1903. Four-mast bark *Schiffbek*, Captain Heinz Jolles

PORT BLAKELY

36   Port Blakely, 1900. Left to right: four-mast bark *Queen Elizabeth*, Captain C. E. Fulton; five-mast schooner *Louis*, Captain Gedburg; four-mast barkentine *Jane L. Stanford*, Captain Mollestad; three-mast bark *Highland*, Captain Smith; four-mast ship *Lancing*, Captain F. W. Chapman; four-mast schooner *Prosper*, Captain Johanssen; steamer *Horda*, Captain Svendsen; three-mast ship *Brodick Castle*, Captain O. Olson; four-mast schooner *Wm. H. Smith*, Captain Smith; three-mast ship *Pera*, Captain A. Teschner; three-mast bark *Seminole*, Captain Taylor; four-mast schooner *Excelsior*, Captain Burmeister; three-mast schooner *Peerless*, Captain Johnson
38   Port Blakely, 1903. Left to right: three-mast ship *Henry Failing*, Captain Graham; four-mast schooner *Bainbridge*, Captain Englebretsen; three-mast barkentine *Newsboy*, Captain A. E. Chipperfield; four-mast bark *Eilbek*, ex *Moreton*, Captain N. P. Moritzen; three-mast ship *Avanti*, ex *Killean*, Captain R. C. Agerup; three-mast ship *Ardnamurchan*, Captain J. McGee

40   Port Blakely, 1905. Left to right: three-mast barkentine *Katie Flickinger*, Captain E. Seel; four-mast schooner *Blakely*, Captain P. Baumann; four-mast ship *Lancing*, Captain S. B. Johnsen, far right
42   Port Blakely sawmills, date unknown
44   Port Ludlow, 1895
46   Port Blakely, 1903. Three-mast ship *Ardnamurchan*, Captain J. McGee; three-mast ship *Avanti*, ex *Killean*, Captain R. C. Agerup; four-mast bark *Eilbek*, ex *Moreton*, Captain N. P. Moritzen
48   Port Blakely, 1901. Four-mast bark *Drummuir*, Captain C. Armstrong; three-mast bark *Lota*, Captain Clayton
50   Port Blakely, 1899. Five-mast schooner *Snow & Burgess*, Captain P. Martensen
51   Port Blakely, 1902? Four-mast schooner *Wempe Bros.*, Captain J. W. Aspe
52   Port Blakely, 1899. Left to right: three-mast schooner *Maweema*, Captain H. A. Smith; four-mast barkentine *Wm. Carson*, Captain J. Piltz; four-mast barkentine *Charles F. Crocker*, Captain H. C. Lund; three-mast bark *India*, Captain C. A. Rohman; three-mast bark *Prussia*, Captain J. P. Hansen; three-mast bark *Plus*, Captain W. Schröder
53   Port Blakely, 1899. Mill tug *Favorite*
54   Port Blakely, 1904. Four-mast bark *Tinto Hill*, Captain E. Jones
55   Port Blakely. Vessel, date, and master unidentified
56   Port Blakely, 1899. Four-mast bark *Ancyra*, Captain J. B. Stuart; four-mast bark *Port Stanley*, Captain H. Williams
57   Port Blakely, 1895. Three-mast ship *Persian*, Captain J. S. Carnegie
58   Port Blakely, 1905. Three-mast ship *Port Logan*, Captain W. Adam; three-mast bark *Prussia*, Captain L. Jensen

141

59 Port Blakely, 1895. Three-mast ship *Persian*, Captain J. S. Carnegie; three-mast ship *Benicia*, Captain T. K. Crammond
60 Port Blakely, 1898. Three-mast ship *Parchim*, Captain J. M. Jacobs
61 Port Blakely, 1900. Four-mast ship *Lancing*, Captain F. W. Chapman
62 Port Blakely, Hall Bros. shipyard, 1902. Left to right: five-mast schooner *H. K. Hall;* four mast schooners *Blakely* and *Caroline*
63 Port Blakely, Hall Bros. shipyard, 1902. Launch of five-mast schooner *H. K. Hall*
64 Port Blakely, Hall Bros. shipyard, 1899. Left to right: Schooners *Wm. H. Smith, Winslow,* and *Lottie Bennett*
65 Port Blakely, Hall Bros. shipyard, 1901. Log boom under construction

TACOMA

66 Tacoma, 1901. Four mast bark *Placilla, Captain O Schmidt*
68 Tacoma, 1901. Four-mast bark *Clan Galbraith*, Captain G. E. Barker
70 Tacoma, 1901. Four-mast bark *Queen Margaret*, Captain R. Logie
72 Tacoma, 1901. Three-mast ship *Claverdon*, Captain R. V. Kelway
74 Tacoma, 1901. Four-mast bark *Lyderhorn*, Captain I. D. Weston
75 Tacoma, 1901. Three-mast ship *Tamar*, Captain J. C. Amberman
76 Tacoma, 1899. Three-mast ship *Hutton Hall*, Captain R. S. Thurber
77 Tacoma, 1902. Three-mast ship *Whitlieburn*, Captain S. Stephens

SHIPS

78 Tacoma, Commencement Bay, 1901. Three-mast ship *Edenballymore*, Captain J. Kendell

80 Tacoma, Commencement Bay, 1899. Four-mast bark *Manchester*, Captain S. Forrest
82 Tacoma, Commencement Bay, 1903. Four-mast bark *California*, ex *Walter Wilson*, Captain G. W. Doty
83 Tacoma, Commencement Bay, 1904. Four-mast bark *Samaritan*, Captain H. H. Dexter
84 Tacoma, Commencement Bay, 1903. Four-mast bark *Forteviot*, Captain W. R. Kidd
85 Tacoma, Commencement Bay, 1899. Four-mast schooner *Endeavour*, Captain W. J. McAllen
86 Dockton, Vashon Island, 1915. Four-mast bark *Svithiod*, Captain Lödin
87 Dockton, Vashon Island, 1903. Four-mast bark *Prince Robert*, Captain C. Hansen
88 Tacoma, Commencement Bay, 1903. Three-mast bark *Admiral Tregethoff*, Captain W. Pund
89 Dockton, Vashon Island, 1898. Four-mast bark *Marion Frazer*, Captain J. MacDonald
90 Tacoma, Commencement Bay, 1902. Four-mast barkentine *Makaweli*, Captain T. Nielson
91 Tacoma, 1904. Four-mast barkentine *Thos. P. Emigh*, Captain M. A. Ipsen

DECK VIEWS

92 Tacoma, Commencement Bay, 1895. Three-mast ship, *Ariadne*, Captain J. Ohlthause
94 Port Blakely, 1904. Four-mast bark *Lisbeth*, ex *Pendragon Castle*, Captain Kaak
95 Tacoma, 1903. Three-mast ship *Cortez*, Captain P. Crosby
96 Port Blakely. Vessel and date unidentified
97 Tacoma, 1903. Four-mast bark *Bermuda*, Captain E. O. M. Korff
98 Tacoma, 1903. Four-mast bark *Mozambique*, Captain R. McCrone
99 Tacoma, 1902. Three-mast ship *Belford*, Captain W. C. McKinnon
100 Tacoma, 1904. Four-mast bark *Wandsbek*, ex *Ancyra*, Captain Kohnke
101 Tacoma. Vessel and date unidentified

102 Port Blakely, 1903. Five-mast schooner *George E. Billings*, Captain J. A. Anderson
103 Tacoma, Commencement Bay, 1903. Four-mast bark *Alsterberg*, Captain E. R. R. Neef

CAPTAINS AND CREWS

104 Tacoma, Commencement Bay, 1899. Four-mast bark *Andelana*, Captain George W. Staling
106 Tacoma. Vessel and date unidentified
108 Seattle, 1903. Three-mast bark *Turgot*, Captain Cézard
110 Port Blakely, 1905. Four-mast bark *Lynton*, Captain E. Gates-James
111 Port Blakely, 1897. Four-mast bark *Kate Thomas*, Captain W. Thomas
112 Tacoma, 1901. Three-mast ship *Boadecia*, Captain T. Lewis
113 Tacoma, 1899. Three-mast ship *Lady Isabella*, Captain W. Jones
114 Port Blakely. Vessel and date unidentified
115 (left) Port Blakely, 1905. Four-mast bark *Lynton*, Captain E. Gates-James
115 (right) Port Blakely, 1901. Three-mast bark *Pera*, Captain Alex Teschner
116 (left) Tacoma, 1903. Four-mast bark *Kinrosshire*, Captain A. McKinnon
116 (right) Tacoma. Vessel and date unidentified
117 Tacoma. Vessel and date unidentified
118 Port Blakely, 1905. Four-mast bark *Lynton*, Captain E. Gates-James
119 Tacoma. Vessel and date unidentified
120 Tacoma, 1902. Three-mast bark *Lamorciere*, Captain Tréhondart
121 Tacoma, 1905. Three-mast ship *Flottbek*, Captain Georg Cringler
122 Tacoma, 1905. Three-mast ship *Flottbek*, Captain Georg Cringler
123 Port Blakely. Vessel and date unidentified

SHIPMASTERS' CABINS

124   Port Blakely, 1905. Four-mast bark *Lynton,* Captain E. Gates-James

126   Tacoma. Vessel and date unidentified

128   Port Blakely, 1903. Five-mast schooner *George E. Billings,* Captain A. Anderson

130   Port Blakely, 1903. Three-mast ship *Cleomene,* Captain W. Learmont

131   Tacoma. Vessel and date unidentified

132   Port Blakely, 1902. Three-mast bark *Abyssinia,* ex *Loch Ranza,* Captain A. W. Hilton

133   Tacoma, 1905. Four-mast bark *Pegasus,* Captain J. Moulton

134   Port Blakely, 1905. Four-mast bark *Lynton,* Captain E. Gates-James

135   Port Blakely, 1905. Four-mast bark *Lynton,* Captain E. Gates-James

136   Tacoma, 1903. Three-mast ship *Eva Montgomery,* Captain G. Harrison

137   Tacoma, 1903. Three-mast ship *Eva Montgomery,* Captain G. Harrison

138   Tacoma, 1904. Four-mast bark *Balmoral,* Captain J. E. Roop

139   Tacoma, 1904. Four-mast bark *Forteviot,* Captain J. Finlay

NOTES

140   Port Blakely, 1905. Four-mast bark *Lynton,* Captain E. Gates-James

144   Port Blakely, 1902. Three-mast ship *Othello,* Captain C. J. Waldbuhn

Page 144: Certain that a waiting ship will quickly fill the empty berth alongside his vessel at Port Blakely, the mate of the Chilean bark Othello *has wisely hoisted his work boat to the port cathead out of harm's way.*